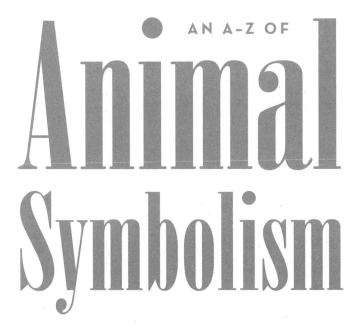

AN A–Z OF

# Animal Symbolism

AN A–Z OF

# Animal

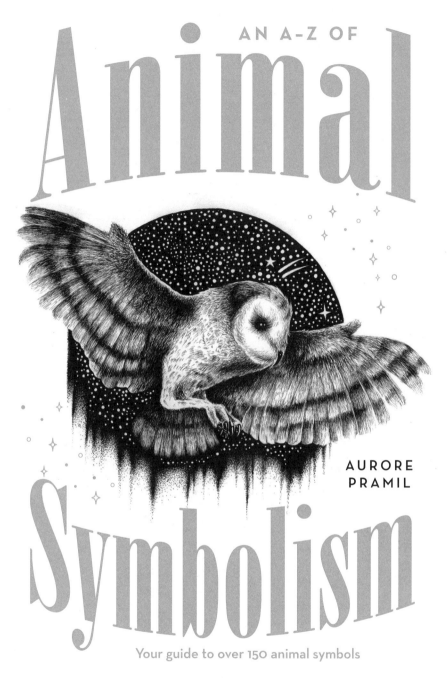

AURORE
PRAMIL

# Symbolism

Your guide to over 150 animal symbols

ROCKPOOL

A Rockpool book
PO Box 252
Summer Hill
NSW 2130
Australia

Rockpoolpublishing.com
Follow us! **f** 🅞 rockpoolpublishing
Tag your images with #rockpoolpublishing

First published as *Dictionnaire des messages des animaux*
© Hachette-Livre (Le Lotus et L'Éléphant) 2022 under ISBN 9782019463991
This edition published in 2024 by Rockpool Publishing

ISBN: 9781922786272

Typesetting by Christine Armstrong, Rockpool Publishing
Translated by Geraldine de Vries
This edition edited by Lisa Macken

A catalogue record for this
book is available from the
National Library of Australia

Printed and bound in China
10 9 8 7 6 5 4 3 2 1

# Contents

## Legendary animals

## Dual animals

# Introduction

It all began with the many, many requests I was receiving from students and patients wanting to know the meaning of an animal presence in their dreams or hoping for an explanation for a particular synchronicity. These inquiries were arriving at all hours of the day – and sometimes of the night! – to the point that I began to sense a deep, universal need to understand these signs. I realised I wanted to share what these animals were telling me so I could pass on their wisdom to the greater number.

I knew that this was an ambitious project because I didn't want to confine the work to totem animals: I wanted to talk about the entire animal kingdom. I also knew that the information I channelled would not always be positive, but that the messages shared by the animals would always be in their image and thus authentic. They do have a sense of humour, and I often laughed during the intense months of channelling work. I hope you will sense some of that joy and lightheartedness in these pages.

I want to underline that each animal in this book confirmed its wish to participate in this project. I felt that I was co-creating with life itself, that my role was one of messenger and translator. My wish to deliver something as credible and accurate as possible sometimes made me doubt my legitimacy as spokesperson for so many living beings, so I tried to remain humble and aligned with their energy.

You'll notice that several of the entries in the book are shorter than the rest, simply because during the writing process some animals had longer exchanges with me than others. Also in this book you will find messages from mythical creatures and dual animals: these are animals that have a particular message and the names of which reflect some of their physical characteristics.

In all of the messages I have channelled the animals speak of the human condition and the questions you tend to have on your mind. These messages are always filled with care and compassion for the difficulty of living your human incarnation; however, the animals won't always tell you what you want to hear. They are not here to flatter your ego but to help you move forward thoughtfully on your life path. You will sometimes be happy to receive an encouraging sign confirming that you're on the right track, while at other times the animals will deliver deeper teachings for you to explore because that is really how you learn. Don't we always learn the most from our hurts and mistakes? These messages may open avenues of reassessment and release to clear your way ahead.

Don't be surprised if you are also offered guidance on your way forward. The animals wish you well and want you to be able to hear their messages, so let them become your guides!

## SYNCHRONICITY

In the 1940s psychiatrist Carl Gustav Jung described the phenomenon of synchronicity as 'the simultaneous occurrence of at least two events showing no causal link but whose association takes on meaning for the one who perceives them'. Synchronicity often revolves around animals, and it triggers strong emotions or feelings that open up the people who experience them to unusual perceptions, strengthening the relationship between the subtle planes and reality. This book aims to help you move deeper into this phenomenon so you may further decode the events in your life and tie them to tangible messages.

## Here are a few examples of synchronicity:

✧ You think of someone, and that person phones you or sends you a text message that same day or at that very moment or you run into them in the street.

✧ You have a question on your mind and request a sign for confirmation, and you suddenly come upon a lovely feather as though it's an answer to your question.

✧ At a dinner someone brings up the topic of magnetism and you find a flyer for a magnetiser in your mailbox, see a TV show that talks about burn healers and someone nearby hurts themselves and asks you to help them. After these multiple instances of synchronicity you finally make the link and understand the meaning of the message: you are being asked to learn to use the energy in your hands!

✧ There are also times when you will feel the openness of the universe even though a situation you're in seems blocked. Events will occur one after the other in the same day or week with messages, encounters and opportunities, as though there was a perfect timing at hand synchronising those events.

There are many other situations that can be qualified as synchronicity. The important thing is that the simultaneous occurrence echoes in you and has meaning for you. It must cause a physical and emotional resonance in you.

## SIGNS FROM NATURE

A sign from nature is a gift from the subtle realms trying to support us in our personal evolution. These signs are often sent to us by animals, but they can also come from a rainbow, tree or rock. Any element can communicate with us and send us messages. This book, however, focuses exclusively on the messages that animals try to bring to our attention.

## ANIMALS AND THEIR POWERS

The true power of animals is in their ability to help us recover our own power and to understand that we can take action for our well-being and freedom. We are actors, not spectators, in our lives.

In animal communication we see the extent to which animals read us like books. Animals have access to our entire beings, our memories and wounds. The simple presence of an animal can sometimes be enough to trigger a new awareness that will enable us to release things that obstruct our paths, and when we discover the magic in these subtle exchanges the phrase 'We are all connected' takes on full meaning. Animals are here to show us that, in the end, there is no boundary between reality and the subtle realms.

# How to use this book

The point isn't to open this book every time you see an animal, because if you try to interpret everything you will disconnect from reality. The book will provide you with useful insights in the following instances:

✧ *You experience a synchronicity or a surprising encounter with an animal*: that animal has come to you to communicate a message from your soul.

✧ *An animal regularly crosses your path*: for instance, if a robin comes to see you every day it most likely has a message for you, which you can look up in the book.

✧ *You are in a particular emotional state and an animal crosses your path*: that animal is most probably bringing you an answer to your questions.

✧ *You dream of an animal or it comes to you in meditation*: you can look up that animal's energy in its description in the book, as well as the awareness it has come to help you absorb.

✧ *You dream of a dead animal or one crosses your path*: this may also deserve an interpretation.

## HOW TO INTERPRET A MESSAGE FROM AN ANIMAL

For each animal in the book the description will provide its energy, which is the element with which that animal is associated, and its season. These factors influence the kind of assistance animals come to bring us (see those sections below for further information). You will also learn the characteristics of each animal and its main message. If you don't have a specific question, this first guidance may be enough for you to grasp what you are meant to hear.

If you do have a question related to particular areas in your life – relationships, work, family and health – you will also find answers pertaining to these themes. Finally, the description for each animal provides special messages and true stories to help you refine your interpretations of your animal encounters.

The important thing is that the message resonates with you and that you find meaning in it. Trust your intuition to help you grasp the scope of the guidance in the deepest parts of your body, and thank the animal that has appeared to you. If the message doesn't make particular sense, set it aside. It's possible that it wasn't meant for you or that understanding will come to you later. Use your feelings to sift through the information and keep only what you do feel concerns you personally.

## ANIMALS AND THE ELEMENTS

SPIRIT ANIMALS: spirit is related to the 'Aum', the sound that created the universe. From that vibration, fire was born. Animals with spirit characteristics travel between worlds and have access to different levels of awareness, from the physical body to the subtle bodies that make up the soul. These animals often appear to people who have the ability to feel the complex resonance of the world.

FIRE ANIMALS: fire is a purifying element that transforms matter and thoughts. Animals with fire characteristics help you overcome strong emotions in need of healing like anger and resentment, so these animals often appear to people who need to find their way forward and transcend their past. Forgiveness is the energy of a fire that, far from being destructive, brings warmth to the heart. Such a transformation is possible with fire animals as allies.

EARTH ANIMALS: earth is your cradle, the place from which all life springs. Many animals carry the energy of earth, with the capacity to bring you back into the present and help you ground your thoughts in reality. These animals come to support people who need to develop greater self-confidence so they can assert their true selves. Earth animals teach you to be bold and stand with both feet on the ground, and to work in collaboration with the energies of the earth.

WATER ANIMALS: the planet and your body are made up of more than 50 per cent water. Animals with water characteristics support the emotional side in you that processes all the information you receive throughout the day. They often appear to sensitive people who have trouble dealing with the emotions of others, and can also help old emotions rise up to the surface so that you may become aware of them.

AIR ANIMALS: animals with air characteristics help you take a step back in a situation and think from a new perspective. They are also connected with the skies and, by extension, with your spirit guides. These animals can be messengers from ascended masters.

## ANIMALS AND THE SEASONS

AUTUMN ANIMALS: in autumn trees divest themselves of their leaves, now useless, to prepare for winter. They accept that they must die just a little so they may be reborn in the spring with new leaves. Animals that embody the energy of autumn help you release the past so you can move on to the next cycle.

WINTER ANIMALS: winter is the season during which nature is at rest and takes time to prepare for fresh life in spring. This break allows seeds, which will bear fruit later on, to prepare for germination. Winter animals help you take the time to think and take stock before a new beginning, as such introspection is often necessary.

**SPRING ANIMALS**: spring is the season of love, renewal and fertility. Life blossoms and sparkles everywhere. Animals that carry the energy of spring help you move forward, dive into new projects and enjoy life.

**SUMMER ANIMALS**: summer is the season of harvests, the time when nature offers her fruits and abundance to the world. Animals that embody this solar energy urge you to contribute your thoughts, energies and ideas to this abundance. It is time to reap the fruits of your hard work.

# ANIMALS CLASSIFIED BY ELEMENT

| Water | Fire | Air (wind) | Earth | Spirit |
|---|---|---|---|---|
| Beaver | Bee | Bumblebee | Ant | Amoeba |
| Camel | Boar | Butterfly | Badger | Bat |
| Carp | Bull | Buzzard | Bear | Blackbird |
| Crab | Dragon | Cicada | Centaur | Cat |
| Crayfish | Eel | Dove | Centipede | Dolphin |
| Crocodile | Fly | Eagle | Cow | Dragonfly |
| Duck | Fox | Egret | Deer | Giraffe |
| Flamingo | Goldfish | Falcon | Doe | Hummingbird |
| Frog | Griffin | Firefly | Dog | Lamb |
| Hippopotamus | Jaguar | Goldfinch | Donkey | Lizard |
| Jellyfish | Lion | Goose | Elephant | Mosquito |
| Kingfisher | Lynx | Grasshopper | Ewe | Octopus |
| Otter | Panda | Greenfinch | Goat, billy | Owl |
| Pelican | Panther | Heron | Goat, nanny | Owl, barn |
| Pike | Pheasant | Hoopoe | Green shield | Peacock |
| Raccoon | Phoenix | Ladybird | bug | Pigeon |
| Salmon | Salamander | Magpie | Groundhog | Raven |
| Seagull | Scorpion | Monkey | Hedgehog | Scarab beetle |
| Seahorse | Tiger | Nightingale | Hen | Starfish |
| Seal | | Ostrich | Horse | Stork |
| Shark | | Parrot | Hydra | Tortoise/turtle |
| Siren | | Praying mantis | Jay | Unicorn |
| Snail | | Red kite | Kangaroo | Wolf |
| Sole | | Robin | Koala | Woodpecker, |
| Stingray | | Song thrush | Llama | green |
| Swan | | Starling | Mole | |
| Toad | | Swallow | Mouse | |
| Trout | | Tit | Pig | |
| Whale | | Vulture | Rabbit | |
| | | Vulture, | Rat | |
| | | bearded | Rhinoceros | |
| | | Woodpecker, | Rooster | |
| | | great spotted | Slug | |
| | | | Snake | |
| | | | Spider | |
| | | | Squirrel | |
| | | | Stick insect | |
| | | | Weasel | |
| | | | Woodlouse | |
| | | | Zebra | |

# ANIMALS CLASSIFIED BY SEASON

| Winter | Spring | Summer | Autumn |
|---|---|---|---|
| Badger | Bat | Ant | Amoeba |
| Bear | Blackbird | Bee | Boar |
| Beaver | Bumblebee | Camel | Bull |
| Carp | Butterfly | Centaur | Centipede |
| Cat | Buzzard | Cicada | Crocodile |
| Eagle | Crab | Cow | Deer |
| Falcon | Crayfish | Dog | Doe |
| Goat, nanny | Dove | Dolphin | Donkey |
| Griffin | Dragonfly | Dragon | Flamingo |
| Groundhog | Duck | Eel | Fox |
| Hen | Egret | Elephant | Hedgehog |
| Lynx | Ewe | Firefly | Hydra |
| Magpie | Frog | Fly | Jaguar |
| Octopus | Grasshopper | Giraffe | Jellyfish |
| Ostrich | Greenfinch | Goat, billy | Mouse |
| Owl | Green shield bug | Goldfinch | Pig |
| Owl, barn | Heron | Goldfish | Pigeon |
| Panther | Hippopotamus | Goose | Raven |
| Pelican | Hoopoe | Horse | Red kite |
| Pike | Jay | Hummingbird | Seahorse |
| Raccoon | Lamb | Kangaroo | Seal |
| Rat | Lizard | Kingfisher | Snail |
| Rhinoceros | Llama | Koala | Squirrel |
| Scarab beetle | Mole | Ladybird | Starling |
| Seagull | Monkey | Lion | Stork |
| Shark | Otter | Mosquito | Weasel |
| Snake | Panda | Nightingale | |
| Starfish | Peacock | Parrot | |
| Tit | Rabbit | Pheasant | |
| Vulture, bearded | Salmon | Phoenix | |
| Whale | Siren | Praying mantis | |
| Wolf | Slug | Robin | |
| | Song thrush | Rooster | |
| | Spider | Salamander | |
| | Stick insect | Scorpion | |
| | Swallow | Sole | |
| | Swan | Stingray | |
| | Toad | Tiger | |
| | Trout | Tortoise/turtle | |
| | Unicorn | Woodpecker, great | |
| | Vulture | spotted | |
| | Woodlouse | Woodpecker, green | |
| | | Zebra | |

# Animals and their messages for you

# Amoeba

Element: **spirit**
Season: **autumn**
Keywords: **curiosity, inner unity, cells**

Amoebas are very intriguing creatures to scientists: neither animal, plant nor fungi, they actually possess characteristics from these three groups. Amoebas live in moist undergrowth and are unicellular organisms with more than one nucleus. Their energy is imbued with curiosity and, incredibly, they can learn and are capable of passing on information. As a matter of fact, amoebas have a lot to teach you. Humans and animals are made up of cells in charge of regulating specific heart, liver or kidney functions but amoebas teach inner unity, the feeling of peace that comes upon you when all the dimensions of your being work in the same direction.

## MESSAGES

An inner conflict could be resolved if you took the time to study what is sparking tensions in you. Is it related to a difficult choice, feelings or principles? Take the time to see more clearly into the issue, then choose a direction aligned with your innermost being and proceed full steam ahead. When you direct all your energy and attention towards a single path you will trigger the power of the law of attraction.

### Relationships

*If you are in a relationship*: curiosity and the desire to learn and share are things that enable a relationship to bloom. It is by discovering the richness of your partner's world that you can open yourself up to a true connection, then you'll be able to create your own common world together.

*If you are single*: what do you really want? Part of you wants to meet someone, but another doubts and cherishes your freedom. It is this duality, this inner conflict, that is preventing change. Perhaps love and independence aren't incompatible, or perhaps you need to make a choice. To resolve this conflict you must determine which part carries the most weight.

## Work

You are torn between your work life and your family as though you had to choose, and this inner tension is disrupting your desire to move forward in your career. Release the guilt you feel in enjoying your work, and make sure to provide true moments of attention to your family. In this way you will reconnect with harmony and love in your heart.

## Family

Your family life requires you to juggle several different roles – in your private life, at work, with your partner, as a parent – and you feel overwhelmed by everyone's expectations. The amoeba has come to teach you the importance of taking your place in the present moment, of settling into each of your roles without thinking of everything else. This is how you will be able to enjoy many different moments without pressuring yourself.

## Health

You are trying to do everything at the same time and exhausting yourself in the process. Multitasking has its limits; managing too many things at once is impossible. Free up some time for yourself, ask for help and accept your physical limits.

## SPECIAL MESSAGES

### If you see an amoeba

An inner conflict is making you tired. To recover your energy, take stock of all your questions and restore your inner peace.

### If you are raising an amoeba

Your curiosity is your greatest asset. You thirst for discovery and learning will take you where you want to go. Keep that energy intact!

# Ant

Element: **earth**

Season: **summer**

Keywords: **social order, father, authority**

Ants are hard workers, dedicated to bringing their societies forward into the future. On an individual level the tasks accomplished by ants may be minuscule, but on the collective level they all contribute to the life of the anthill. Ants accept social order, for they know that without a framework and rules the clan's organisation would be bound to fail. The ant invites you to reflect on the issue of authority and on how you relate to the father. In their societies ants submit to the will of their queens and work for the development of their communities.

## MESSAGES

A part of you may be rebelling against the education you received. This desire to defy authority pushes you to fight for what is right for you and for others. You want to help, on a social level. However, beware of excesses: having respect for rules is paramount for social order. You must find your happy medium, and your education has given you the tools to make a place for yourself in society.

### Relationships

*If you are in a relationship*: the way you relate to authority has some importance in your love life. You sometimes feel a desire to rethink your relationship to break social norms, and on other occasions you feel comfortable in that framework. You could try to find some peace, somehow, so you can walk your own path without guilt. You can always infringe on certain rules and abide by others; there is no need to throw everything out. Each anthill has its own organisation, and what counts is that you find happiness in your own.

*If you are single*: you may be fleeing certain types of partners that remind you too much of your father or another authority figure. It's normal for some things to manifest in your partners, and these shouldn't make you bolt from deeper relationships. Everything is not always black or white, and you are not your parents. It is up to you to reinvent your standards.

## Work

You hate monotony and are afraid of becoming bored in your job. You need challenges, and to feel that things can grow and change. Be bold, acquire new skills or undertake a skills assessment to find your place or a way to grow. Don't forget that in an anthill, every single worker is important. If one is missing, the operation of the entire colony is imperiled. Don't play down your role!

## Family

You are like an ant going the wrong way. You are not always understood by your family, who wonders about how you function. There is no need to oppose everything: sometimes life will simply invite you to change rivers and let yourself be carried by the current. If you spend your life fighting you will burn yourself out. Try to be a bit kinder with yourself, as it would help you soothe buried anger.

## Health

An inner struggle or conflict of some kind is eating you up and preventing you from fully enjoying your life. This energy is obstructing your digestive system, the function of which is to process not only food but also emotions. Seek out what truly matters to you and put a little peace of mind into it. It will help.

## SPECIAL MESSAGES

### If you find an anthill in your garden

Your yearning for emancipation resonates with a quest for an ideal. You want to create your own way of life, another reality. If there are many of you to collaborate, everything is possible.

### If you have ants in your house

There is a conflict revolving around your place in the family that you have to resolve, because it is keeping you from moving forward in the way you'd like. You act from a place of rebellion or submission, but in reality you are not free. Give yourself permission to live outside of this conflict.

### If you find yourself sitting on an anthill

This unfortunate occurrence invites you to question your relationship with yourself from the point of view of authority. You may perhaps ask too much of yourself?

# Badger

Element: **earth**
Season: **winter**
Keywords: **stores, survival, scarcity**

To survive the winter badgers draw nourishment from their stores of fat. The badger symbolises the spare tyre we all more or less need in case of difficult times. For some people this will be a layer of belly fat, and for others it will be money put aside. This power animal comes to you if you are afraid of scarcity, questioning you about this fear that puts you in constant survival mode.

## MESSAGES

A deep fear of scarcity emphasises your need for security. You are searching for love or money, and may even sometimes confuse both. The badger comes to show you that your fear isn't entirely founded. Unlike badgers in the winter, you are not in danger. Soothe your worries and develop a lighter relationship with your body and money.

### Relationships

*If you are in a relationship*: your emotional dependence sometimes causes you to act immaturely. You are very demanding with your partner, despite not being clear about your true needs. At the root of things you are dominated by your fear and it is polluting your relationship. Take stock of the need that pushes you to always expect more of your partner, and speak with them about it to ease the situation.

*If you are single*: your body is in protection mode. Putting on weight is a way of keeping potential partners at bay and maintaining emotional distance between you and the outside world. Becoming aware of it is the first step towards releasing your fear.

## Work

At work you either pile up the hours without counting your efforts, or you take it easy for long periods of time. This modus operandi works well for you, enabling you to harness your energy and then to rest and think of other things. Just take care not to fall asleep and miss the train when it is ready to leave again.

## Family

Your relationship with money and your worries in this area come from old family fears and memories of real scarcity. Separate the past from the present so you can relax your inner tension.

## Health

When it's operating on survival mode your body slows down, its metabolism and functions decelerate to save energy and stores build up in the event of scarcity. Your thyroid can also be impacted by this fear and slow down its activity.

## SPECIAL MESSAGES

### If you see a badger

A fear of scarcity needs to be brought to the surface of your awareness. By embracing it, you will be able to integrate it and overcome it.

### If you see a dead badger

You are in the process of releasing certain fears and progressing with greater serenity on your path. The badger encourages you to leave aside your old modus operandi and trust in life.

# Bat

Element: **spirit**
Season: **spring**
Keywords: **hidden side, shadows, revelation**

Bats have fascinated us since the dawn of time, giving life to fantasies and stories. They have often been associated with the vampire myth and morbid energies due to their attraction to blood. In reality, bats reveal the hidden sides of our personalities. On the path to self-knowledge it is much easier to go towards the light than towards the shadows, yet the shadows are precisely where great light lies. The bat invites you to visit the hidden side of your conscious mind, where the key to your freedom resides.

## MESSAGES

In the depths of your conscious mind there is an underworld, an abyss in which all your fears are stored. Learning to walk the path towards self also means facing what may be concealed in these places, and discovering why you didn't want to see it. This is the key to knowing your innermost being, and through that you will be able to observe all your parts, shadow and light, for one cannot exist without the other. Your shadow parts are the best possible support for the expression of your light. Instead of fleeing from them, learn to make them your allies.

### Relationships

*If you are in a relationship*: revealing your weaknesses and vulnerability to your partner isn't an easy thing, yet you are that dual and imperfect being. You would gain in mutual trust if you lifted the veil on all the parts of who you are.

*If you are single*: it is only human to want to show yourself to your best advantage, but no one is made only of light. The bat supports you to observe others in their duality. Choosing a truly self-aware person is a guarantee of trust. On their own path, that person will have tamed their shadow part.

## Work

Self-knowledge can help you find your career path or the reasons for your troubles in that area. You need to accept the fears that prevent you from achieving your potential. The problem has nothing to do with your skill set, but with the fact that a part of you is silently sabotaging them.

## Family

Family is often at the heart of inner conflicts and unconscious truths. It is where you find your strengths but also your weaknesses. Everything isn't black or white, and you need to learn to discern the balance that could emerge from that heritage.

## Health

Fear is an invisible enemy. The way your body operates is directly influenced by this emotion, for it turns the lock on your kidney functions and energy. Your fear can become your ally, however, because it conceals a desire. By making more room for that desire in your life, the energy in your kidneys will be released and your fear will dissolve.

## SPECIAL MESSAGES

### If you see a bat at night
You are about to receive a vision or have a dream that will provide you with insights into an unconscious desire.

## If you see a bat in the daytime
Do not be afraid of your own light. You can bring all the parts of who you are into harmony by getting to know yourself better.

## If you dream of a bat
It is time to embark on a deep process of introspection to unearth messages from your subconscious.

# Bear

Element: **earth**
Season: **winter**
Keywords: **introspection, territory, courage**

The bear symbolises introspective energy and the ability to take stock and live in accordance with the seasons. Bears are also creatures with which there can be no negotiation: their territory is theirs, end of story! This power animal embodies quiet strength with the talent to assert choices with wisdom and courage. The bear's knowledge is grounded in its strong connection with nature and capacity to explore its territory, driven by curiosity and an appetite for life.

## MESSAGES

You know what you want but you don't dare carry it out. 'Enough!' says the bear. Be bold, and bang your fist on the table to make your voice heard. Trust in your curious nature: it is instinctive but also connected with your self-knowledge and understanding of your experiences, and it will lead you in new directions. There is a time for everything, and after introspection and maturation the moment has come to take action.

### Relationships

*If you are in a relationship*: taking a break would enable you to recharge your energy and implement common projects. You are stronger together. The bear invites you to work together on your future by pooling everything you both know.

*If you are single*: curiosity is not an ugly flaw. It is your desire to enjoy a life to the fullest that has you looking for love and brings you so many positive feelings. Don't be afraid: with the bear as your ally you will be able to avoid obstacles from the past.

## Work

Your experience has enabled you to acquire knowledge that you now need to use wisely to go where your curiosity wants to take you. Don't stop wanting to learn and develop your skill set, because it is by maintaining an open mind that you can discern where the best opportunities lie.

## Family

Your family is your cave, your refuge where you can go to rest, but after a while the yearning to explore and enjoy life will resurface and be stronger than anything else. You know that you can leave your loved ones for a time and then, if you feel the need, go back to warm up beside them.

## Health

Bears take time to enjoy life. Don't work too hard. Ease off the gas pedal, and pay attention to the yearnings communicated by your body. Allow yourself more pleasurable moments, or your body will end up notifying you of its needs but differently through pain or illness.

## SPECIAL MESSAGES

### If you dream of a bear

When a bear comes to you in a dream it is to help you regain your self-confidence. Nothing is impossible; everything is a question of wanting and listening. If you follow that path you will be able to move mountains!

### If you see a bear

What new areas would you like to explore? It is time to venture into them.

# Beaver

Element: **water**
Season: **winter**
Keywords: **dexterity, creativity, dream job**

Beavers are builders, and this power animal will appear to you if you are good with your hands and invite you to make your dreams come true. Building, inventing, creating and transforming are the key words of these incredible animals. Nothing stops them, especially not water! This element, which beavers have mastered to perfection, is connected with the emotional realm. The beaver will appear to you if you are a creative person who needs to overcome your fear so you can dive into your passion.

## MESSAGES

You yearn to do something with your hands and feel that it could be a great source of joy in your life. However, changing direction and moving towards unknown waters is an equation that cannot be resolved without fear. The strength of the beaver is here to support you, and show you that with a little willpower you can overcome any obstacle and, especially, free yourself from the emotions that control you.

### Relationships

*If you are in a relationship*: a homemade gift is so much more precious than a store-bought object. Use your talents to make something that will please your partner because, in doing so, you will understand that creating is a present you give to others but also to yourself.

*If you are single*: you are going to meet someone who shares your passion. Make contact with a society or group in your field of interest for this alchemy to come to life!

## Work

For beavers, this is the heart of the matter. You need to use your hands to be happy in your work, as your kinesthetic sense needs to be in action so you can release pleasure hormones. You can become depressed without a form of manual activity.

## Family

Your gift for creation is a heritage passed down by one or more members of your family and needs to find means of expression in your life. The more you give it room, the more you will beam with happiness!

## Health

You are in solid health, so nurture this energy and know how to use it wisely. Your mental health depends on your opportunities for action.

### If you discover a beaver dam

Emotions are taking precedence over your projects, so don't let your fears command your future. Starting projects will open your heart and activate a sparkling energy inside, and it is this energy that will help you overcome your emotions.

### If you see a beaver

You have a talent for conception and creation, a gift that must be given room in your life.

### If you dream of a beaver

A project currently on hold is asking to be heard. Don't shut away the creative part of who you are or you could miss your life purpose.

# Bee

Element: **fire**

Season: **summer**

Keywords: **collective intelligence, universal love, interdependence**

Bees are one of those species that are crucial to human survival. Their ability to work for the greater good of the world goes beyond anything you can comprehend. They are driven by complete, unconditional love, transforming everything they touch into nectar and fruit. Bees have an interconnected relationship with flowers and strong ties to floral energy, and many trees owe their survival to bees. This power animal invites you to open your heart to unity. The honeycombs in a beehive are built on principles of sacred geometry: take the time to observe this magic and you will be impressed!

## MESSAGES

How does your heart vibe: with your family, in your work or in society in general? What do you do for the greater good? The bee urges you to enter into the vibration of 'one': the vibration of the universe, of infinite love. If you do not yet feel that you are in this energy, ask the bee to keep guiding you. You can use high-quality honey to connect with this manifestation of love in the material world. Let the nectar flow inside you and bring light into your personal hive. Become aware of the fragility of this balance, which we all need to preserve through our actions. When you open your awareness to all life on earth you will find your rightful place.

## Relationships

*If you are in a relationship*: the bee invites you to engage in a stable and sustainable relationship so you can create your own hive. You can start working on long-term projects, which will bring you harmony.

*If you are single*: embrace this possibility in your heart, and what you hope for will soon manifest in your life.

## Work

Your hard work and attention to detail are soon going to pay off and you will be able to reap the fruits of what you have sown. Your work has had an impact beyond your immediate environment and your qualities have benefited others.

## Family

Harmony and peace in the home are paramount to you, so you must do everything you can to make them a priority. Don't let work take precedence over friends and family.

## Health

Your vital energy is a precious thing, so don't waste it on useless quests. Focus on what brings you joy and serves your mental and physical well-being. Floral energy through the use of elixirs or Bach flower remedies can help you resolve small nervous disorders.

## SPECIAL MESSAGES

### If you are stung by a bee

It could mean you need to review your priorities and start focusing on the greater good. It is time to appease any tensions that may exist in your family. The bee's venom has excellent protective properties, and you will resolve your conflicts. In the event of an allergic reaction it would be a good idea to explore any toxic memories in your family.

**If you find a swarm of bees around your home**
Your home is filled with gentleness and love. You have created a harmonious environment and the bees have connected with your positive vibrations. They are watching over your family. Don't forget to thank them before calling a beekeeper to retrieve them.

## A NEW HIVE

Séverine, a friend of mine who is phobic about bees, was parking her car in front of my house when a migrating swarm appeared in front of her. No bees came into the car because she managed to close her windows in time, but she was in a state of panic. This is the message I received for her: 'Life wishes you well. If you are not happy where you are, change the location of your hive or create your own.' At the time Séverine had a lot of questions on her mind and was wondering if she should start her own business. She embraced the very positive sign that was given to her that day, and now she is the proud owner of a flourishing business.

# Blackbird

Element: **spirit**
Season: **spring**
Keywords: **messenger of spirit guides, signs, announcements**

Blackbirds are allies in your everyday life, facilitating contact with the subtle realms. They carry messages from spirit guides who work alongside you. The blackbird appears when you need to take time to observe the signs around you and open your mind to this magic. In its own way the blackbird comes to urge you to pay attention: the subtle realms are trying to get in touch with you.

## MESSAGES

The blackbird has come to announce that your spirit guides are preparing a message for you, a message that will be brought to you very soon and will be important. The blackbird urges you to be receptive to anything you might see, hear or dream of in the days and nights to come. Do you have a particular question on your mind? Have you made a particular request? If not, you are invited to consciously embrace what will present itself to you. If you did set an intention you should receive guidance to give you direction.

### Relationships
*If you are in a relationship*: something is in the works, and an event you were waiting for is about to happen. 'It is on the way,' is the blackbird's message for you.

*If you are single*: you may have a feeling of a long wait when you want change to come into your life. The blackbird has come to prepare you for the movement you have been waiting for, because your message has been heard and its resonance will be with you soon.

## Work

The blackbird invites you to make more room for intuition in your work, and to let yourself be carried by the signs you may perceive. The blackbird will be your ally to enable your activity to exist on a spiritual plane.

## Family

If you have recently lost a loved one they might come to you in the shape of a blackbird. It's as though they are trying to attract your attention to communicate a message. Listen to your feelings, as they will guide this reconnection.

## Health

Your body takes on a role of expressing unsaid things and repressed emotions. The blackbird asks you to listen to any pain you may feel in your body or any illness you may have as a message from your subtle body. In other words, your soul finds expression through your body and your body is your soul's best messenger!

## SPECIAL MESSAGES

### If you see a blackbird sing

You will soon receive a message from your spirit guides in audio form: through the radio, a conversation with someone, a TV show or a voice in a dream. Pay attention and listen!

### If a blackbird lands in your garden or on your balcony

You are going to receive a message, and it will be important. Be ready and keep an open mind, because any means of communication is possible. A heart forewarned is a heart prepared, and you will recognise the message when you get it.

### If you dream of a blackbird
Your spirit guides are with you and keep trying to show you the way. The blackbird supports you in preparing to receive a message.

### If you find a dead blackbird
Someone who has passed on to the other side is trying to contact you and has been wanting to send you a message for a long time. Open yourself up to embrace their vibe.

# Boar

Element: **fire**
Season: **autumn**
Keywords: **earthly energy, grounding, present moment**

Boars love to turn over the earth in their search for food. Their energy is very grounding, and they help the people they meet to stay in touch with reality and avoid escaping into their thoughts too much. The boar draws its strength from the here and now, bringing sacredness and the present moment into harmony on earth.

## MESSAGES

You often have your head up in the clouds and are a little disconnected from others, not really here but not really elsewhere either. Real life is sometimes too hard, and you prefer to escape in order not to suffer too much. You feel the presence of your guides but only in your spirit, and that refuge has become a golden cage from which you would now like to exit. The boar has come precisely to help you stay grounded. Connection with spirit exists in the material world, in real life and in the power of the present moment.

### Relationships
*If you are in a relationship*: your lack of groundedness can sometimes be a little difficult to live with for your partner. You forget a lot of things, lose your belongings and don't really seem to be present in your moments together. Learn to set aside your preoccupations so

you can be in a true attitude of sharing. Your relationship needs real time for listening and exchange.

*If you are single*: fantasies are important, as they keep desire alive along with a yearning to learn more about another person. However, they must not become a refuge that prevents you from meeting someone important. Perfect people only exist in mushy movies. Your romantic nature won't prevent you from finding the right person as long as you are willing to accept other people's flaws.

## Work

To see a project through it is best to focus on concrete goals. Dreaming may seem useful before diving in, but once you are on your way you need to be well grounded to move quickly towards your goal.

## Family

Your family relationships can sometimes be troubled and you prefer to escape or avoid hard discussions, yet facing problems and giving voice to them can also give way to a healthier family dynamic. Instead of fleeing when the atmosphere becomes charged, make it easier to breathe by releasing unsaid things.

## Health

Your lack of groundedness can lead you to push back the good resolutions you made to improve your health. You want to do it and you know how to go about it, but you can't seem to manifest it in the present moment. Instead of facing a problem one step at a time you have a tendency to go around it by dreaming. You need to understand the mechanisms that defeat you so you are able to set realistic goals and achieve them.

## SPECIAL MESSAGES

### If you see a boar

Groundedness is your weak point. You have ideas, so don't just hang about dreaming about them. Take action!

### If a boar comes into your garden

Your relationship with your spirituality is too abstract. Spirits live in the subtle and invisible realms, but they guide you to understand the sacred nature of life on earth. If you are made of blood and bone, it is to experience spirituality in your real life.

# Bull

Element: **fire**
Season: **autumn**
Keywords: **duality, charisma, strength**

The bull's energy goes two ways: on the one hand these are impulsive creatures that are dominated by their hormones, and on the other they possess innate wisdom and charisma. Bulls show natural authority, supported by their strong, powerful nature. A bull reassures and contains its herd, and represents the duality of the masculine principal in search of evolution.

## MESSAGES

When you really want something you can actually be quite bull headed. That tenacity is an asset, for it enables you to build your projects despite any obstacles that come your way. However, this asset must not be detrimental to the people around you. If you can learn to demonstrate natural, benevolent authority you will obtain what you want.

### Relationships

*If you are in a relationship*: you react too quickly sometimes and then regret your outburst. Your impulsive behaviour plays tricks on you. Take time to think before leaping into action and you will avoid hurting your partner without meaning to.

*If you are single*: your power and self-assurance attract potential partners. The sexual tension is tangible, but don't get lost in it! A part of you is also looking for stability, so don't forget that.

### Work

You feel a need to take matters into your own hands in order not to have to deal with higher management, and you have what it takes to be a leader. Setting yourself up as self-employed could allow you to be fully free to do as you like.

### Family

Your natural authority can sometimes be disturbing to strong characters, who tend to oppose your way of being. If you are looking to resolve a conflict, forget force: use your charisma to communicate that this is not your fight. You sometimes mistake personal challenges for ego wars, so don't take everything so personally!

### Health

You can be subject to mood swings and rises in testosterone, adrenaline and noradrenaline, which increase your reactiveness and sensitivity to stress. On a sexual level your strong drive leads you to take risks, so don't forget to use protection.

## SPECIAL MESSAGES

### If you dream of a bull

Yearnings are rising up inside you, and they want to be heard. Your personal power is increasing; know how to use it wisely.

### If you see a bull behaving calmly

You radiate beautiful harmony. You can on occasion let your spirited nature express itself, but you always know how to bring others towards collective success.

### If you are charged at by a bull

You don't make use of all the potential you have inside you. Don't forget that a positive leader is, first and foremost, a kind person who uses their charisma wisely.

# Bumblebee

Element: **air**
Season: **spring**
Keywords: **peaceable, dreams, ambition**

Bumblebees have great strength but never use it, and are peaceable creatures that seek dialogue rather than conflicts. Their wings can make an impressive sound because it is through the power of that sound that they indicate their presence. These insects have dreams and see things through to the end; not knowing that something is impossible, they just go ahead and do it. From a scientific point of view the size of a bumblebee's wings compared with the weight of its body should make it impossible for it to fly, yet bumblebees don't even think about it: they just go ahead and fly! Perhaps not entirely gracefully or discreetly, but they do go where they want to in their own way. The bumblebee is at the service of its soul.

## MESSAGES

You are an extrovert, someone people hear talking from afar who laughs a lot. You have the gift of creating a warm and friendly atmosphere, you attract others like a magnet and you're a good friend, someone others can count on. Beyond your kindness you are a dreamer, and ambitious. The bumblebee invites you to believe in your dreams: you have the capacity to make the impossible possible!

### Relationships

*If you are in a relationship*: your sympathy factor and warmth have charmed your partner. You know how to create a pleasant atmosphere in your home, and your presence brightens the house. Your partner feels secure by your side.

*If you are single*: you have a lot to offer but sometimes a potential partner sees you as just another friend. Put your mediation talents to good use so you can move your game pieces forward and communicate your intention to charm.

### Work

Positions of responsibility suit you well because your charisma and ability to bring others into your projects create an atmosphere of trust. You like challenges, and you need a serene environment to meet them. You are invited to coordinate everyone's strengths and turn trial runs into success stories.

### Family

As a child your head was sometimes up in the clouds, but now this aspect of who you are is your biggest asset. Your imagination is boundless and you can do whatever you like!

### Health

You have a lot of strength and energy; nature has gifted you with a body that enables you to go wherever you like. Be grateful for this gift and take good care of that vehicle of yours. You have the potential to go far.

## SPECIAL MESSAGES

**If you see a bumblebee**

Your innate kindness is a gift for others. Don't change that about yourself just because you find yourself faced with a conflict. Also, don't change to adapt to the world; rather, create your own world in your image.

### If a bumblebee comes into your house
What dream have you set aside that is now ripe to be revived?

### If a bumblebee flies into your window
The way before you is clear and there are no obstacles; it is all in your head. You have all the capacity you need to go through walls and attain your goal.

# Butterfly
## (and caterpillar)

Element: **air**
Season: **spring**
Keywords: **metamorphosis, creativity, poetry**

Butterflies symbolise inner and outer transformation in the way a caterpillar turns into a gorgeous butterfly. The butterfly sings an ode to life and the beauty of nature: who can remain unmoved by its charm? Poetic souls take flight with the butterfly towards a world of dreams.

## MESSAGES

The butterfly invites you to make more room for your imagination and know that the creative process happens inside as well as outside you. An inner transformation will enable your talents and imagination to run wild.

### Relationships

*If you are in a relationship*: daily life isn't always easy. Don't wait for Valentine's Day to celebrate your love and relationship. Plan for a rendezvous in nature, and let the poet inside you find ways of expression to charm your partner.

*If you are single*: you have already known more than one metamorphosis in your life and you know that spreading your wings in a new way requires time. This time, which you will allow yourself to experience alone, is favourable to discovering new paths for inner transformation. Your heart wants to display its colours. The way is being paved for you, so trust in the process.

## Work

You are looking for a way to express your creativity in your activities. Your imagination is letting loose, so how can you make good use of it on a professional or personal level?

## Family

Enjoy life and moments of sharing and joy without thoughts of tomorrow. Everything moves constantly, but with the butterfly what counts is the present moment. It is up to you to seize its magic.

## Health

Nothing is fixed. Your body isn't inert but is full of life and feeling, and it is connected with your thoughts and energy. The butterfly's magic is in its ability to transform its body to show its beauty. If you have personal insecurities the time has come for a metamorphosis, perhaps a simple change in look or taking ownership of who you are and finding yourself beautiful. Put yourself in alignment with your innermost being: it is the greatest gift you can give yourself!

## SPECIAL MESSAGES

### If you see a butterfly flitting around
There is poetry in the present moment and it is here, so embrace it. In its magic, a deceased loved one could send you a sign.

### If a butterfly lands on you
It is time to awaken your imagination and set it in motion. Find a path of exploration to reveal your talents.

### If you encounter a rare butterfly
An opportunity is going to present itself, and you will have to seize it without giving way to doubt. It will be a sign that you're on the right track.

### If a butterfly comes into your home

You could let your creativity find a means of expression in your home by changing the colour of your walls or renovating old pieces of furniture. Transforming your home will help you transmute your outer image.

### If you find a caterpillar

You are paving the way for a great change in your life. Be patient for it might take time, but in the end you will spread your wings and take flight. Don't neglect this essential step, as everything comes to those who know how to wait for it.

## THE BUTTERFLY'S LESSON

This guidance was given to Laurence by her totem animal, the butterfly. 'I wanted to launch an activity I had set my heart on but I was overwhelmed by fear and doubt. Was I really capable of making that change? Would I be able to support my family? I went for an energy-healing session to obtain some guidance and I received a message from my totem animal, the butterfly. It told me: "Life is unpredictable, but each stone you remove from your path will give you more space and lightness so that you can bring more flexibility into your life. It is when unexpected or disruptive events present themselves that you have the greatest potential for evolution. I am your butterfly, Laurence. I help you take flight and bring poetry into your life. I am the multicoloured butterfly in your dreams, and I help you leave your chrysalid so that you can spread your wings in the world."'

# Buzzard

Element: **air**
Season: **spring**
Keywords: **reassessment, life review, choices**

Buzzards are similar in their characteristics to eagles, but while the latter stay high up in the skies buzzards know how to get closer to people. This makes them more appealing and easier to listen to. The buzzard guides you towards a necessary reassessment or life review before overcoming a hurdle or making a choice. This power animal helps you remain aligned with your heart and values, and especially to not let yourself be influenced.

## MESSAGES

We all experience times of reappraisal and the need to make life choices, so it may be time to think about taking a short break to take stock. Are you satisfied? What are your priorities? Remaining aligned with your values is a form of personal success. The buzzard encourages you to continue what you are doing to prevent the outer world from influencing the choices of your heart. You are on the right track to find your place on earth.

### Relationships

*If you are in a relationship*: taking stock of your place in your relationship, your projects and what you want enables you both to remain aligned on the same path. Take time to reflect together, work on your common plan and readjust your points of view in accordance with your new priorities.

*If you are single*: before making a change, ask yourself what brings you to experience this situation. Is it something you want or something you have to endure? Do you feel well with it? What would you like to find or transform? The buzzard supports you in this phase of questioning and is guiding you towards your heart truth.

### Work

Your desire to be useful and give meaning to your actions sometimes comes up against the reality of your workplace. The buzzard is helping you see how you could compensate that lack through a complementary activity, or think about making a change in your career path to better align your work with your values.

### Family

You are not always in agreement with your family on topics like education or your way of life. This isn't a problem; your choices are yours. Just be true to yourself, as this will enable you to send reassuring signals to your loved ones even if they don't share your values. Take care to speak kindly when you are in disagreement. All points of view are possible, and differences must be respected.

### Health

Your health is your most precious possession. Without it, there is not much you can contemplate doing. Remember to take care of yourself and avoid oxidative stress. If you feel unhappy in a situation, see how you could make things better. There must be some solutions that can alleviate your anxiety.

## SPECIAL MESSAGES

### If you see a buzzard sitting still

Before making a choice, allow yourself to take a break and rethink your past experiences so you can better understand what is motivating your decision. A level of self-confidence is necessary for momentum to rise when you make a choice. Outer influences can make you doubt, which is why you must never lose sight of your primary objective.

### If you see a buzzard flying high in the sky
Your head is all cluttered up, and no good decision can be made in such a muddle. Take a break for the weekend and return to thinking about your situation once you've gained some perspective.

### If you see a buzzard flying very low in the sky
Something needs to change for you to align your life with your thoughts and values, and there are most likely some choices to be made to clear the way ahead.

### If you find a dead buzzard
It is time to take stock of your current situation so you can be sure you're not on the wrong path. Look at the signs around you to stay on the right track.

## RECASTING A NEW PATH

Before embracing the calling entrusted to me by animals I had a private practice as a nutritionist. I was on the point of setting up another activity centred on well-being, and a friend who was also a partner in this project and I were on our way to a supplier when we began to see dead buzzards on the side of the road. After 10 such occurrences we decided that this really made for a lot of coincidences. The meaning of this experience was soon revealed to me: I needed to drop the well-being project to start working in the support of animals. It was a difficult decision for me to make at the time because it involved embarking on an uncertain path, but soon after I was able to reassess and recast my situation.

# Camel

## (and dromedary)

Element: **water**

Season: **summer**

Keywords: **water guardian, survival, environment**

Camels are water guardians that have adapted to their habitat and found ways to tap into their survival abilities. Camels teach you that when you take care of your energy you can survive in hostile environments. The water they retain inside them symbolises the pure emotions you can preserve in difficult situations.

## MESSAGES

When the camel appears it means you have gone through a difficult situation. You might not yet be completely out of this conflict and it is always easy to give way to anger, but you are under the protection of the camel and they want you to keep faith. A shining future awaits you beyond your current problems, so preserve your desire to smile and enjoy life.

### Relationships

*If you are in a relationship*: you are going through ups and downs in your relationship, which is perfectly normal. The important thing is to know that your love is still intact. Everyday problems can sometimes make you forget what first brought you together – the love you share – but remember that love when the going gets tough.

*If you are single*: like a long trek through the desert, solitude can sometimes lead you to be fooled by a mirage. Don't forget that the source of love is inside you, and that you already possess everything you need. Your quest for a relationship must not lead you to deceive yourself with illusions. Your future partner is a beautiful surprise waiting for you in an oasis so keep going, because you are going to meet someone.

## Work

Money is like the water present in a camel's body: abundance is inside you. The camel asks you to believe in your capacity to avoid scarcity and obtain everything you need. Be bold, and ask to be paid at the height of your true worth.

## Family

Your ancestors found ways to go on in the face of adversity and have passed that strength down to you. You are capable of overcoming this difficulty whatever the cost, and you will maintain that beautiful light deep inside you.

## Health

Sickness and death are hardships that can sometimes make you lose faith in life. Camels have inner resources, and so do you. The camel supports you in seeing that these resources are still present inside you and that life is the strongest force of all!

## SPECIAL MESSAGES

### If you see or dream of a camel

You are being asked to protect all of your inner resources.

### If you see or dream of a dromedary (a one-humped camel)

The message here is more nuanced: you are invited to cultivate your positive energies.

# Carp

Element: **water**
Season: **winter**
Keywords: **secrets, ancestors, freedom**

Carp often bring their heads out of the water and give an impression of wanting to speak, but no words come out of their mouths. This probably accounts for the saying (in French): 'Silent as a carp.' (The equivalent saying in English is 'Silent as the grave.') The carp's energy brings us back to unsaid things, to the matters our ancestors took with them without being able to express them. The carp brings up to the surface from the deepest depths of our subconscious the desire to speak up. These fish bring good luck, because when we free our speech we free the generations to come of the heavy influence of their ancestors.

## MESSAGE

We live in a world where social norms allow us to say things that in previous times were inadmissible. The carp invites you to speak up for your ancestors, who were unable to do it for themselves. Whatever the reason that made them keep their secrets, it is time to free your speech to enable the energy of sound to move and flow for yourself and your entire line.

# Cat

Element: **spirit**
Season: **winter**
Keywords: **spirit world, intuition, subtle dimensions**

Cats have the ability to see what cannot be seen. The subtle realms have no secrets for them, and they know how to connect with energies beyond your plane of reality. Cats also work to keep energies in balance in their homes and within their humans. The cat appears when you need to call upon your intuition. This power animal acts as a catalyst that propels a human's world towards a much more vibrant dimension and, in so doing, enables that human's perceptions to become more intense.

## MESSAGES

You know that when you listen to your intuition you are never wrong, yet you still have trouble trusting in yourself every day. The cat supports you in this encounter with yourself. The truth is out there invisible to the naked eye, but cats know that beyond reality there is a realm where everything is influenced by the energy it sends out. Learn to see the vibrant world that surrounds you.

### Relationships

*If you are in a relationship*: like a cat, you like to be with your partner but you also sometimes need to be alone. These moments of calm give you an opportunity to rebalance your energy, and they are indispensable to your personal equilibrium.

*If you are single*: cats are solitary, self-sufficient animals. This alone time you are experiencing is important, because through it you must learn to appreciate solitude. You must first build happiness yourself, then it can be shared.

### Work

One of this animal's many qualities is patience. Cats never rush into things, but wait for opportunities to present themselves. If you are hoping for something to change have faith and pay attention, because an opening will show you that the time has come for you to act.

### Family

You perceive the state of mind of the people you love. You can even from a distance feel if something has happened to them. This ability is called intuition. It is not only in the important moments that you must listen to it; you also need to learn to trust yourself in your daily life.

### Health

Your health is connected with the state of your energy. By learning to restore the energy in your body, like a cat knows how to do for itself or for you, your body will feel less of a need to express itself through physical disorders.

## SPECIAL MESSAGES

**If you see a cat**
Your intuition is correct. Keep going in the same direction!

**If you find a lost cat**
You are invited to devote more attention to the spirit world in your life to restore balance in your energy.

### If a cat comes into your house

The energies in your home need to be rebalanced. The cat has come to help you raise the frequency of your living space.

### If you dream of a cat

You are opening doors to intuition and perception. The cat will be your guide on this path of initiation.

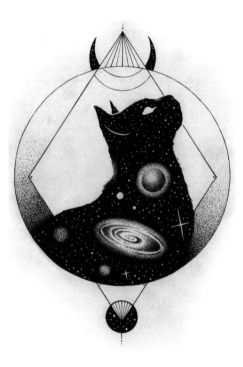

# Centipede

Element: **earth**
Season: **autumn**
Keywords: **creativity, direction, consistency**

Centipedes coordinate all their many legs to move in a single direction. This power animal supports creatives in all their diversity. If you are a singular person with a tendency to scatter your focus in your artistic world you can ask the centipede to help you converge your skills towards a single goal.

## MESSAGE

You may be a person who brims with dreams and ideas but has trouble taking action. The centipede wants to show you that all your passions can be brought together and directed towards a unique aim. You have a great many qualities, and you could try to unite them for better congruence and efficiency.

# Cicada

Element: **air**

Season: **summer**

Keywords: **friendship, sharing, relationships**

Cicadas brim with solar energy and love to share their zest for life, and they sing to open up your heart. Cicadas are hedonistic creatures that remind you that life is only worth living in the company of good people. Friendships are important to this power animal.

## MESSAGE

You need to reconnect with the warmth of a welcoming home by opening your door to the people you love. The cicada invites you to bring sharing and exchange into your daily life on an even more present level. Social, joyful and genuine relationships are one of your driving forces.

# Cow

Element: **earth**

Season: **summer**

Keywords: **Mother Nature, comfort, earthly nourishment**

The cow represents the maternal, nurturing spirit of Mother Nature providing abundant nourishment for her children. The cow's energy embodies absolute comfort and the possibility of stopping for a moment to take universal love fully inside you as nourishment.

## MESSAGES

Earthly nourishment is abundant, and knowing how to give thanks for it by choosing quality foods will enable you to maintain a healthy vitality. Remember to give thanks for this abundance and to not eat too much. Excesses will clog up your body and hamper your vitality.

### Relationships

*If you are in a relationship*: if your partner is still hanging on to their mother's apron strings, the time has come to help them become aware that the heart of their existence is now within your own family circle. If you are the one with rather too-strong ties to your mother, try to find reassurance in the fact that you are now that central energy building a relationship and a family.

*If you are single*: love is a part of life's abundance, and you feel a desire for someone who would fill your heart with their presence. Is this a need, or a lack? Do you feel the need for a partner who would share the events of life by your side or are you looking for someone who would heal your wounds? A pot full of holes cannot be filled; your heart needs to be repaired for you to be able to embrace abundance in love.

## Work

Your performance at work is directly connected with the food you ingest. Take stock of your eating habits so you can optimise your vitality and concentration. Take a real break for lunch with a catnap or a short meditation to be full of energy for the afternoon.

## Family

Your emotional ties to certain members of your family are very strong, and you watch over these people. Like a universal mother, you pay attention to your little ones and find great joy in this role. Your involvement is all to your credit, but remember to disconnect yourself from time to time so you can take a break and rest for a bit.

## Health

Your body does not handle certain foods well. Try to see which might be causing you digestive trouble, and select the ones that benefit you the most so you can rebalance your nutritional intake.

## SPECIAL MESSAGES

### If you see a herd of cows
You need to recharge your batteries, so plan a calm, restful weekend.

### If a cow charges at you
It is time to take some distance from a family member for greater freedom, otherwise that connection could become toxic.

### If a herd of cows is blocking the road
Take stock of your eating habits. Fasting for a few days will help restore your liver's detoxification capacity.

# Crab

Element: **water**
Season: **spring**
Keywords: **exchange, materiality, human condition**

Crabs owe their survival to their pincers, which are completely oversized compared with their legs. Those pincers are like our hands: indispensable. Crabs are in an energy of giving and receiving, and this teaching will remind you of your ability to rethink the world along lines of greater solidarity. The crab invites you to divest yourself of material excesses so you can receive differently, through emotion. What can you do with your hands to better the human condition? See how children play with crabs' pincers and the souvenir the crabs leave them with as they try to escape from those clumsy little hands.

## MESSAGES

You have accumulated objects and other material possessions you don't need, so sort through your belongings and reconsider your priorities. The crab invites you to consider what really matters to you; it can be just as lovely to give as it is to receive. Does that energy of exchange flow in your life? What could you change for a better experience of your presence on earth? In other words, what can you improve for yourself and others?

### Relationships
*If you are in a relationship*: we can all give a hand to help make the world of tomorrow a kinder place. Compassion and sharing can

be beautiful projects, and making a donation or participating in a charitable project will give meaning to your relationship.

*If you are single*: perhaps the one you are looking for isn't in the sphere of people you are engaging with. If you move towards those who have already given meaning to their lives you will find a partner who vibes on the same level as you.

## Work

Whatever your area of work is you can instil a charitable feeling into your workplace by making room for sharing and solidarity. Be the one who takes the initiative to engage in a cause, and bring everyone together in support of your project.

## Family

Solidarity begins with your family. Exchanging skills and intergenerational knowledge is a precious gift, so take advantage of your elders' presence to learn and, in turn, pass down to your descendants what you have learned.

## Health

Energy is a balanced exchange. If you are only on the giving end you will tire yourself out, so take time to receive as well. Divesting yourself of useless things that clutter up your mind and home will help this exchange to flow. Give away what you no longer need, as it will increase your energy.

## SPECIAL MESSAGES

### If you find an empty crab pincer

If you give your energy away to people who aren't ready to be in a connection of exchange you are likely to exhaust yourself and become an empty shell. Change your approach, and engage in a cause that has meaning for you.

## If you see a crab

You have the ability to bring people together in support of a common cause. You will gain as much pleasure from this as from what you succeed in gathering.

## If you find a dead crab

Solidarity is a priceless vector of energy. Don't forget to make room for it in your life.

# Crayfish

Element: **water**
Season: **spring**
Keywords: **balance, authority, adaptability**

Crayfish are incredibly adaptable creatures that are able to thrive in fresh as well as salt water. However, they can become very invasive and destructive, depending on their environment, so the presence of predators is necessary to maintain a balance in their population. The crayfish reminds you how the milieu in which you grow up is important to your fulfilment.

## MESSAGES

Crayfish speak of authority, which you may sometimes have great difficulty accepting but which will teach you respect, structure and limits. The crayfish reminds you that without a healthy and structuring authority there will be chaos. You need a secure framework to work towards your potential without becoming invasive or unadapted to living in society. Balance in nature is fragile, and all species contribute to maintaining a certain order. When a particular species takes over all others suffer from that despotic authority.

### Relationships

*If you are in a relationship*: one of you may have a tendency to take power over the other, and even be a bit tyrannical. Everything depends on the mutual boundaries you have established, so if you feel that balance is being lost then think about redefining the framework of your relationship. If everything is fine, it is in all likelihood thanks to the good communication you have succeeded in building together.

*If you are single*: do you feel capable of adapting to another person, culture or sociocultural environment? Some relationships require more adaptability than others to function in a healthy manner. How were you raised, and what do you want to pass down in turn? Start by getting to know yourself well so you can then adapt to a partner.

## Work

Be careful! For you, your company or the area in which you work is like fresh or salt water for crayfish: environment changes everything. Do you feel comfortable with your management? Have you established relationships based on dialogue? How do you feel about this authority? A feeling of discomfort may be an opportunity to reconnect with your inner child to see what is going on in your relationship with authority.

## Family

The crayfish speaks to your inner child, but also to parents and future parents who will one day have to think about the education they received and the framework they will build for their own children. Think about the aspects of education that to you seem unadapted to life today and adjust. Don't forget that it is incumbent upon you to help your children find their own place and be respectful towards others.

## Health

Your health comes and goes depending on your state of mind. When you feel good you are full of energy and have strong resistance against viruses, but when you feel depressed or are in the company of toxic people your immune system quickly weakens. The environment in which you live is crucial to your physical and mental health.

## SPECIAL MESSAGES

### If you see crayfish in water

The environment in which you live is healthy, and you have been able to adapt. You know how to show authority when you need to without abusing your power. You are also capable of communicating with your management and expressing your limits.

### If you see crayfish out of the water

There are one or two aspects in your life that deserve an overhaul and your inner child needs reassurance. You need to review the way you relate to authority in your relationships with others as well as in regard to yourself. You can show authority without becoming despotic; it is up to you to find a happy medium.

## HOW THE CRAYFISH MADE ITS WAY INTO THIS BOOK

I had just begun writing when a crayfish appeared in the garden of the house we had rented for our holiday: it had crawled up from the river to signify its desire to participate in this project! What is promised is due, and the crayfish is now included in these pages.

# Crocodile

Element: **water**
Season: **autumn**
Keywords: **depths of the unconscious, self-exploration**

Crocodiles have ties with the planet's seismic movements and connections with the depths of the unconscious. Their very thick skin is like a carapace. The crocodile knows that in order for you to reach deep levels of your being you need to bypass a number of resistances, which are a form of protection established by your mind to block the release of buried truths. The crocodile appears to you if you wish to explore your innermost self.

## MESSAGES

Everyone lives in a reality forged by what they think is true. If you are searching for your true nature, your innermost being, you're on the right track. The crocodile's precious support will help you overcome barriers set up by your mind. Fear is a principal obstacle, as is the unconscious opposition to change. If you lift the veil on these mechanisms you will be able to reach unexplored depths.

### Relationships

*If you are in a relationship*: a number of unconscious fears may be at work, placing barriers in areas of your relationship. If you wish to overcome them you will need to find a way to shed your protective carapace. Without this desire for personal liberation your fears will remain in control of your mind.

*If you are single*: to reach your heart a potential partner had better be patient, because your protection mechanisms are so strong that they act as a repellant without you even being aware of it. The crocodile wants to help you relax your defences. You will see that if you are profoundly at peace in your interactions with others then the energy will be different, as they will come towards you more spontaneously!

## Work

You may unconsciously set up barriers in your career against success, joy, self-worth, challenges and personal abilities. These are reasons to explore the obstacles currently preventing the change you desire.

## Family

Family memories may be at the root of fears or obstacles in relation to your personal fulfilment. A deeper study of this unconscious heritage will help you reach your personal truth by dismantling inherited beliefs.

## Health

The crocodile is associated with the skin part of your body. Skin problems are frequent in people who have not yet lifted all the obstacles preventing their personal liberation. Like a snake shedding its skin, inner change manifests outwardly.

## SPECIAL MESSAGES

### If you dream of a crocodile

It is time to release your carapace, as your innermost being wants to move into the light and take up the reins of your life. This change has been simmering inside you for a long time, and you only need to realise that it can be made to happen for your mind to start making it a reality.

### If you see a crocodile

A buried truth is going to rise up to the surface of your awareness. This will be an excellent thing for you, as it will open up fresh possibilities.

# Deer
## (and roe deer)

Element: **earth**
Season: **autumn**
Keywords: **majesty, yang energy, action**

The majestic deer embodies the energies of both earth and sky, and appears to us to encourage strong grounding and good circulation in our yang or masculine energy to help us take action. Celestial or yin energy descends through the deer's antlers and comes to meet its four anchor points on earth, or yang energy. Everything is a question of self-assurance with this power animal. Intuition must be at the service of the material world, and therefore of your actions. There is no refuge to be found in dreams; it is by taking action that you will find your connection with earth and light.

## MESSAGES

You have a tendency to take flight into your dreams and thoughts to escape reality. The deer brings you back to the here and now, and into your action power. What decision have you been pushing back for a while even though making it would help you feel that you are the master of your destiny? Making choices is an excellent way of remaining in the present. The deer has appeared to tell you that you are absolutely capable of steering your own boat and taking the lead.

### Relationships
*If you are in a relationship*: the buck and doe represent the sacred couple. The deer invites you to make suggestions, to innovate. Don't

wait for your partner to bring you your dream on a golden plate. Make destiny happen by creating surprises!

*If you are single*: you have great action power, and you can decide to open or close the door to your heart. Don't waste time dreaming of Prince Charming, because he only exists in fairy tales. Be realistic in your expectations and open yourself up to the magic of encounters. If you wait too long you will miss out on opportunities.

## Work

The deer is asking you, 'What do you feel?' Stop thinking about the future and enjoy the here and now. You are living an experience and tomorrow is another day, so for now put your energy into the present moment. The deer is helping you focus on your current action, which is where you'll find the energy to build your tomorrow.

## Family

Certain decisions must be taken together, and it is up to you to unite the family around an action you want to take. Use your know-how to bring everyone together around the same single goal.

## Health

Don't go too far in your daydreaming; remember to bring your ideas back down to earth. When you are not well grounded you may feel a little dizzy or lacking in energy. Plant your feet firmly into the ground and breathe in three times to enable yang energy to take its full place in your body.

## SPECIAL MESSAGES

### If you see a deer on the side of the road

Stop for a few minutes and look at how far you have already come. You have learned a lot about yourself, and you have the capacity to experience everything life brings you. Open your heart: it is ready to be filled.

### If you dream of a deer

An idea will come to you and sprout. Receive the energy of the deer, and see in the days or months ahead how this idea becomes more defined in your mind. When it is crystal clear, take action!

### If you see a deer in the bush

You are rebalancing your energies completely. Harmony between your yin and yang now allows you to channel celestial messages and ground them in your reality. The deer thanks you for your contribution on earth.

# Doe

Element: **earth**
Season: **autumn**
Keywords: **universal love, gentleness, kindness**

Does are connected with universal love and embody kindheartedness par excellence. They have the ability to transform anything. Through their gentle eyes, does reveal the inner light that guides you towards a better version of yourself.

## MESSAGES

We all have two sides: a bright side and a shadow part. You are invited to let your steps be guided by light while accepting your duality. Release your fear of loving others, for the doe is taking you into another dimension: one of universal love of life. Find that strength, as it will be your best guide towards a new version of yourself, capable of loving without measure.

### Relationships

*If you are in a relationship*: to love another, you need to be capable of first loving yourself before expecting it of your partner. Then love becomes a gift that you can offer boundlessly, as it exists abundantly in your heart.

*If you are single*: fear of pain can impede love, as can fear of misreading a relationship. The doe invites you to enter into a dimension of love in the broadest sense: the love of life and its magic. This gives love a new meaning through which it becomes an encounter of your own self through your partner.

### Work

Some people hide away what is most beautiful about them, as if that was necessary for self-protection or success. With the support of the doe you can remain centred on your heart vibration so you can attract possibilities and openings. Be authentic! Success doesn't always mean winning, but rather feeling that you are moving forward in alignment with your values.

### Family

Your ties to your loved ones go far beyond what you think. Your ancestors are watching over you, and you are all connected with your clan through the heart. This loving energy is abundant, and you can lean on it when you feel the need.

### Health

Your weak spot is your desire to help. The spirit of the doe reminds you that you cannot help those who aren't ready for it, and that you might exhaust yourself for nothing. Learn to let go and concentrate on what is most important.

## SPECIAL MESSAGES

### If you dream of a doe

Your heart is filled with great, beautiful light. Don't be afraid to move towards what you like best, as it is there that your capacity for love resides.

### If you see a doe

This is a sign of an encounter with your own self through another person. The doe's eyes are seeking out the light in your heart to help banish all your fears. Embrace this energy within you like a gift.

### If you find an injured doe

You have suffered in the past and shut away your heart. It is high time to heal so you can open yourself up to the dimension of love.

# Dog

Element: **earth**
Season: **summer**
Keywords: **unconditional love, attachment, loyalty**

Dogs love without measure, and they offer that love unconditionally. They never judge, are always willing and communicate all the joy they feel in the presence of a human. The attachment of dogs and their unfailing loyalty make them forget their own needs. Acting as a mirror to you if you need to see the difficulty you have in loving, the dog comes to show you how to reconnect with your loyalty so you can let the joy of true love fully resonate.

## MESSAGES

Loving means more than just loving another person or an animal. The vibration of love is a boundless energy that spreads in any circumstance. Love invites you to open your heart to authenticity, including to yourself. The dog comes to prompt you to bring your choices into alignment with your heart.

### Relationships
*If you are in a relationship*: walking the path of life with another person often involves making concessions. The dog is here to help you reflect on what you have set aside so you can be in your relationship. Loyalty towards your partner means you have to be authentic, so if a compromise is weighing on you then express it freely.

# D

*If you are single*: it is possible that unconscious loyalties are making you relive family patterns. Your love affairs follow on the heels of each other and are strangely similar. Know that you can change the course of things; no disaster can repeat itself indefinitely. It is up to you to make yourself available to the resonance in your heart by ending the family cycle.

## Work

You sometimes expect too much from your management and need your work to be validated and recognised. You invest a lot of energy into your job and are sometimes disappointed by what you get in return. Try not to take your work so much to heart, and direct your energy towards people or activities that will offer a more satisfying return.

## Family

Dogs raise the question of unconscious family loyalties. Without necessarily being aware that you do, you perpetuate known patterns to please your clan. Of course, this alienates you from joy and personal satisfaction, because you do things to make other people happy. If there is one person towards whom you should show loyalty and sincerity, that person is you!

## Health

Joy is an emotion that heals many torments. The dog is a real resource to help you find the connection with unconditional love. This energy of light and healing can change your life.

## SPECIAL MESSAGES

### If you find a lost dog
It is time to take care of your personal happiness and recapture joy in life.

### If you see a dog that has been run over by a car

You need to change something, especially in the way you define your priorities and desires. Become aware of the stumbling blocks that bring you to make choices to please others rather than yourself.

### If a dog comes into your house

You will soon be the recipient of good news, and this will bring you joy. Your heart will be filled with love! You have so much to offer . . .

# Dolphin

Element: **spirit**
Season: **summer**
Keywords: **spiritual being, primordial breath of life**

Dolphins are gifted with self-awareness. They travel between the fourth and fifth dimensions, where whales and other animals also navigate. Dolphins help humans become aware of life, and of their spiritual dimension and divine nature. Connected with the inner child, the dolphin takes you back to the essence of your being and helps you recapture the primordial breath of life that was delivered to you at birth so that you can shine on earth.

## MESSAGES

The dolphin is a lightworker, striving alongside awakeners of consciousness: people who have incarnated on earth to support others in their spiritual elevation. If the dolphin appears to you it is most probably time to accept this role that was given to you at birth. Your presence on earth is important, so don't be afraid to embody your values in this world.

### Relationships

*If you are in a relationship*: your partner is sometimes surprised by your nature, and your sensitivity is not always understood. The dolphin has come to help you enter into a phase of acceptance. By gaining in self-confidence you will be able to send out clearer signals to your partner, who will understand your reactions with greater ease.

*If you are single*: more than what you say, your non-verbal communication reveals a lot about who you are and your energy radiates subtle information. The dolphin wants to help you align your verbal and non-verbal communication so that you may appear to the world authentically. Trust in yourself; you are a beautiful person!

## Work

For dolphins life is a game, and work can also be a source of fun for your inner child. Think about how you can adapt your work from this angle to bring more lightness into your life.

## Family

Your soul was not born into your family for no reason. You incarnated on earth to contribute to raising awareness, and this starts with the people closest to you. It isn't always easy and you may have felt misunderstood, but the point isn't to convince others. Remain true to yourself and seek out the path of joy, which is how you will inspire those around you to evolve.

## Health

To be happy you need to be in an environment that understands you. You don't feel very content when you're with people who do not have the same awareness as you, and it can leave you exhausted. Take good care of your energy. By connecting with the vibes of the dolphin you will be able to recharge your batteries.

## SPECIAL MESSAGES

### If you dream of dolphins

You were born to shine out your bright nature. The dolphin has come to help you accept that your body is a vehicle for incredible emotions and sensations. Let them flow through you.

### If you see a dolphin

A wave of joy is reconnecting you with your inner child, the one who knows why you are here. Listen to that child. Something beyond words is aligning in you and you need to let that energy infuse in you.

# Donkey

Element: **earth**

Season: **autumn**

Keywords: **intelligence, beliefs, conditioning**

Donkeys have a different energy from horses. They also evoke freedom, but in the form of freedom of thought. The donkey invites you to reflect on the conditioning that smothers your ability to excel. If you accept as truth what others think of you, you give credit to their beliefs and deny your inner truth. What your heart says isn't always what your head likes to think. What if following your instinct was the truest form of intelligence?

## MESSAGES

You are moulded by your experience, but also by what the world mirrors back to you. The person in front of you is a distorting mirror that does not necessarily reflect your truth, and when you trust in this image you no longer see what shines in you. To find your inner treasure you need to search deep inside your heart, where your passion lies. The donkey urges you to regain confidence in your personal power.

### Relationships

*If you are in a relationship*: some childhood wounds can cause an excessive need to be reassured and validated by your partner. Even if it feels good, don't delegate too much of your power but do trust in your choices. Your partner's opinion may be insightful, but it cannot alter your convictions. Learn to follow your heart.

*If you are single*: you are insufficiently aware of your intellectual abilities and lack self-confidence. Be bold, take your rightful place and stand by who you are. Choose an authentic person capable of discerning your true potential, and shun misplaced egos.

## Work

You are a gifted person. This gifted aspect of yourself needs to be heard, nourished and seen. Begin by accepting it, and understand how important it is to your personal development and fulfilment in your career.

## Family

It is time to release any judgements cast upon you as a child that conditioned your self-esteem. Your abilities are far greater than you think. If you never let your gifts emerge to the light of day you will live in the shadows of your beliefs. You are not what people say you are, but what you want to be! In other words, you are free to reinvent yourself beyond the old ways of thinking of your childhood.

## Health

Your body has an incredible capacity for regeneration, but you need to be aware of it. If throughout your childhood you were told you were weak or fragile or if you were identified as someone who was sickly, then your body will behave in the way that it is expected to. The information contained in your mind conditions the way your cells and immune system function. The donkey invites you to understand that you are your own best medicine. Repeat the following mantra to release your conditioning: 'I honour my body because it is powerful and luminous. I have confidence in my healing capacity and I love my body.' Say this mantra about 10 times, consciously, every day for 21 days so you can activate cellular healing.

## SPECIAL MESSAGES

### If you hear a donkey bray
The time has come for you to release any old hurtful words you may have heard said against you so that your creative potential may bloom and appear to the light of day.

### If you see a donkey
What is blocking you is rooted in something you judge yourself for. You are capable of so much more than you think!

# D

# Dove
## (and turtledove)

Element: **air**
Season: **spring**
Keywords: **peace, luck, love**

Symbols of love and peace, doves are often associated with weddings. They also embody your soul's passage into light, freeing your spirit. Doves are often seen together in pairs. The male is very loyal and is involved in protecting its young. The dove's energy is gentle and peaceful, and when you connect with it you can feel this peace as warmth and soothing in your heart.

## MESSAGES

The dove has come to bring you a message of peace: you are invited to appreciate the calm things in your life. In times of existential crisis, see how lucky you are not to have to struggle to find food and water. The dove supports you in focusing on the simple things.

### Relationships

*If you are in a relationship*: your relationship may be going through a time of doubt and questioning. Know that love and loyalty are present. The love you share is sincere, and it will survive the storms that sometimes blow you about even if they are healthy in the end. The dove has come to reassure you that things are only temporary.

*If you are single*: the dove comes bearing a message of peace, which your heart will find. You need to find what can favour your

84

happiness in your current situation. There are advantages to solitude, so instead of hoping for it to change, rejoice in what you are capable of giving yourself.

## Work

A wind of good luck is allowing you to look serenely towards the future. Take fearless advantage of the present moment. Rejoice, and trust in your lucky star.

## Family

You have a close-knit family, which enables you to savour shared moments and create new memories. Seize this opportunity to see family members who live further away, and organise family reunions. If there are conflicts at the root of your questioning, promote peace by re-establishing dialogue.

## Health

Focus on your heart chakra; there may be energies there to release. Try to discern what needs to be appeased. To find inner peace, the important thing isn't necessarily to heal but to accept. What are you resisting that deserves to be simply accepted as it is?

## A LOVELY CASE OF SYNCHRONICITY

I was in an appointment with a patient and we were talking about having the freedom to let ourselves accept another person as they are on their life path, wherever that may be. At that same moment we saw two doves perched on a branch, facing the window. It was a lovely case of synchronicity!

# D

### If doves are nesting on your property

You are invited to devote your full attention to harmony and warmth in your home, and to strengthen your inner peace.

### If you find yourself tending a dove

You are healing a system of thought, which is allowing you to recover inner harmony. Continue appreciating your good fortune and the path you are on.

### If you see a dead dove

It is time to divest yourself of your good person role. You will never feel better than when you are at peace with yourself and expressing your true personality. Peace doesn't mean agreeing with everybody, but being genuine to yourself. There is no such thing as perfection: be perfectly imperfect!

## APPRECIATING DAILY COMFORT

A pair of doves had decided to nest just above our patio. We had the great fortune of witnessing the birth of two babies, and we watched in wonder as they grew until they were old enough to fly. Living so close to the nest created a connection. We liked to observe their behaviour and how they were coming into their life force. Whenever there was a storm we went to see if the nest was still there, aware of the struggle of these little animals to survive while we, snug and warm in our house, never had to worry about wind or rain. We watched as the parents took turns to sit on the eggs and then feed the chicks. This pair of doves reminded us to appreciate our daily comfort.

# Dragonfly

Element: **spirit**
Season: **spring**
Keywords: **inner transformation, extension of being**

Dragonflies begin their lives as larvae living in water, then they leave the water to begin transforming into their final shape. Every cell in a dragonfly's body is engaged in this process of inner change and the extension of its new body and wings. This incredible transformation takes time: as larvae, dragonflies can spend up to three years underwater. The dragonfly will appear to you if you are engaged in change on a very deep level, with a transmutation of your entire being.

## MESSAGES

You are going to shed your old skin, leave your comfort zone and open yourself up to the world around you. The invisible realms will be where your new being, liberated from its old beliefs, will explore fresh territory. You have been moving towards this deep transformation and engaging in self-work for a long while, and the time has come to leave the water and give birth to your new life.

### Relationships

*If you are in a relationship*: your inner progress is starting to move your partner, and their world of thoughts is evolving. This movement might not yet be perceptible; let time do the rest.

*If you are single*: like a dragonfly, you have spent enough time underwater thinking things through. It is time to leave your maturation space and spread your wings towards a new destination. Shed your old skin to become the person you truly are and leave the past behind you.

## Work

It may be time to change your way of doing things. Processes that have matured to the end can now give life to a new methodology. Whether on an educational, human, material or conceptual level, you have the capacity to redefine your work environment.

## Family

Leaving the nest involves leaning on what has been given while releasing what weighs on you. You have reached that point of balance between what you have received and what you wish to keep. The way is clear for you to leave and freely explore fresh horizons.

## Health

A dragonfly knows that it will need to expend great energy for its final transformation, which is why at the larva stage its primary focus is on nourishment. Food is an essential source of energy, and you are invited to balance your nutritional intake. Make sure to eat healthy foods so you can support your body's evolution towards a higher frequency.

## SPECIAL MESSAGES

### If you see a dragonfly in flight

You are on your way towards fresh horizons. Don't be afraid to venture beyond your current field of knowledge.

### If you see a pair of dragonflies coupling

Love gives you wings! You are going to receive support from someone you love.

**If you see a dragonfly on a body of water**
You have been thinking things through long enough, and it is time to take action! The way is open before you.

**If you see a dragonfly perched on a branch**
You are in a waiting phase. Everything is ready inside you but you don't dare take off. If you look closer you will see that you have already extended your wings. Everything starts with your mind.

# Duck

Element: **water**
Season: **spring**
Keywords: **rites of passage, evolution, inner child**

Ducks represent the energy of transitions, of rites of passage, like when a child becomes an adult. Ducks are present in moments of important change and growth in connection with your inner child, and they potentiate the effect of a rite of passage to enable your soul to align with the person you are at the time.

## MESSAGES

It is possible that a part of you refused to grow up. For its own reasons, your inner child perceived that it would be endangered if it were to become an adult. This attitude may block you somehow now, for the inner child mustn't cut itself away from the emerging adult. There is no danger in growing up, in taking responsibility. The duck wants to give you the opportunity to reconcile the adult and child so that creativity and joy can inspire you in your daily life.

### Relationships

*If you are in a relationship*: owning responsibility in a relationship means accepting that both people do their best for the common good. It means not expecting your partner to understand implicit things, but rather taking the lead to express these things and talk them over together. This is how a relationship can evolve in a balanced way.

*If you are single*: a part of you is afraid of change. This is in relation to your inner child, who refused to grow up. If commitment scares you, perhaps it is due to a projection that is not your own. If you could reassure that child today, what would you tell them?

## Work

The inner child has dreams where the adult has a job. This has created an opposition between work and pleasure, and the resulting everydayness weighs on you and impacts your personal life. Take your inner child with you to work to rediscover that environment with fresh eyes. If this seems impossible to you, start by getting back in touch with your inner child before trying to bring it into the here and now.

## Family

Your parental models and family patterns may have contributed to your inner child having an erroneous view of adult life and refusing to grow up. This is called the Peter Pan syndrome, where you want to retain your child's heart. Rest assured that no one is forcing you to give it up. Become aware that you have a tendency to reject responsibility in situations you nevertheless created yourself.

## Health

A child's heart vibration is one of joy and carefreeness. This emotion wants to sprout everywhere in your adult life to help you forge ties with that little being inside you that is trying to tell you its dreams. Make room for the new you. Don't be afraid to let go of your old habits; you will feel so much lighter.

## SPECIAL MESSAGES

### If you find a duck feather

Duck feathers speak to the inner child. If the feather is small with a white tip it is your inner newborn that needs to be heard. If the feather was shed by a female duck it is your tie to your mother that needs to be explored. If it is a male duck's feather it is your tie to your father. If the feather is all white it is a message of inner peace, and you can release your fears.

### If you see a flock of ducks

It is time to grow up. Stop behaving like a child, and take charge. You are responsible for your own life; you can choose what works for you. Take back ownership of your personal power.

## LOVING YOUR INNER CHILD

One late evening someone rang our doorbell. Surprised, we went to open it and found ourselves talking to a man who wanted to know if the female duck in our garden belonged to us and what we were planning to do with her and her ducklings, for they were a protected species. After trying in vain to capture the duck and her babies we resigned ourselves to the situation, and in the end the mama left of her own free will to pursue her path elsewhere. This incongruous visit came to remind us that we needed to be just as attentive towards our inner child as that duck had been to her little family.

# Eagle

Element: **air**

Season: **winter**

Keywords: **elevation of the mind, materiality, point of view**

Eagles fly high in the sky and possess a broad vision that is also very sharp. They know how to focus on their targets rather than on the details of a landscape. Eagles soar beyond the issues of our world yet are willing to land to give birth to a new generation. The eagle is a journeyer, capable of exploring fresh territory, and urges you to elevate your mind. You are invited to stay in touch with material reality so you can build your life, all the while rising above the superficiality of your problems.

## MESSAGES

Curiosity is the first key given to the mind in search of a wider field of investigation. You yearn to open the door to renewal, as though you are being urged on by a supernatural gust of wind. Spirituality is trying to find its place in your life, so trust in the guides that come to help you.

### Relationships

*If you are in a relationship*: it is natural to want to take a step back. By allowing yourself this distance you will be able to better discern what you can improve in your relationship or, simply, what you like about your partner.

*If you are single*: setting down your luggage and building your own nest is at the heart of your concerns. Let yourself be carried by the wind to new places so that you may meet your ideal partner. By rising above and gaining perspective you will widen your view and potentiate your chances of success!

## Work

Inspiration strikes when the mind slips away. The eagle invites you to go on a journey in your head and explore new horizons. Lightness of mind and personal distance will enable you to see more clearly into your projects and focus better on your goals. Meditation could help you find the necessary inner calm before diving into action.

## Family

Your family is your bedrock, what helps you keep your hold on reality. You may sometimes lose your grounding because you are too connected with the skies and not enough with the earth. Your ancestors and your line are your earth. Even if real life is sometimes more difficult to live in than voyages of the mind, it is very good for you. Take time to rest in it by being in the present moment.

## Health

Resting your mind is crucial to rebuilding your energy. You think a lot, sometimes too much. Take advantage of some meditation time to fly with the eagle, rising above your life and problems so you can attain another, more objective point of view.

## SPECIAL MESSAGES

### If you dream of an eagle or are visited by one during meditation

Your mind is taking flight. Trust in the new horizon taking shape before you. The vision you have of life is going to evolve, and you are supported in this awakening.

# E

**If you see an eagle in the sky**
Your soul is trying to communicate important information concerning your innermost identity, your essence. Pay attention to any signs that come your way.

## THE SHAMANS' FRIEND

The eagle often comes to meet people engaged in a shamanistic practice and guides them on the spiritual path. The eagle may also represent a benevolent ancestor watching over your soul travels. This power animal is always the instigator of an awakening of the mind and heart towards a reality free from superficiality. It also brings awareness of how deeply you can truly communicate with other people.

# Eel

Element: **fire**

Season: **summer**

Keywords: **hypersensitivity, obstacles, protection**

Although eels are water-dwelling creatures, electric eels can produce electricity if they feel threatened. As they don't have a spiny dorsal fin and only small teeth they seem harmless at first glance, yet they possess a formidable mechanism of defence. The adage about the quiet ones being the ones you need to look out for is particularly appropriate when describing the eel, a clever animal that knows how to tame its emotions so it can channel its inner fire and confront the other carnivores living in deep waters.

## MESSAGE

If you have been hypersensitive since birth, feeling capable of confronting others can be a real challenge. The people around you may worry about your 'oversensitivity', as they like to label it. The energy of the eel is now coming to help you, and once you accept your inner power as a gift you will be well able to map out your path. Like the eel you will have the ability to intelligently weave between life's obstacles, and in the event of attacks on your energy you will be able to call upon your talents to dissuade ill-intentioned people. You can vibe in alignment with your heart and not let others pollute your life!

# Egret

Element: **air**
Season: **spring**
Keywords: **ally, mutual aid, living together**

Egrets are a common bird that can easily be observed in fields alongside cows and horses. The great egret and little egret alike cohabit with other species, benefiting them by ridding them of their parasites. This beautiful white bird comes to remind you that you need an ally. Learning to live together with people's differences and sharing with others are challenges you must address. The egret urges you to join forces in fair mutual aid.

## MESSAGES

You may like to believe that you can manage on your own, but a need to be supported by others sometimes contradicts this assurance. Your desire to go it alone is so entrenched that you no longer know how to ask for help when you need it, yet you have done a lot for the people around you and they are waiting to do the same in return. You won't lose your independence by soliciting solidarity and mutual aid from others.

### Relationships

*If you are in a relationship*: living with another person means accepting your mutual differences and turning them into assets. Of course, you don't always share the same tastes and wants but you can count on each other. Your complementarity is what gives your relationship strength.

*If you are single*: you would like to meet someone, but living in a relationship scares you a little because your solitary life works for you and your freedom is important to you. You don't need to think of living together at first; you can start by getting to know each other better. All forms of relationships are possible, even long distance, as long as it suits both partners.

## Work

Your job brings you to collaborating with people from different professions than yours. Don't minimise the impact of this collaboration. People who don't possess all your skills are very important to your future. Be aware of all the forms of assistance the universe brings you, and don't forget to give thanks.

## Family

Intergenerational mutual assistance is a gift you should not ignore. Find your place within your community by making yourself useful and extending your generosity. You will receive as much as you give.

## Health

The help of a kindhearted person in your immediate environment will be beneficial to you, be it to take a walk and chat about your lives or to let that person give you a hand for an odd job. Any form of aid will relieve the burden you carry from always wanting to do things alone.

## SPECIAL MESSAGES

### If you see an egret alone in a field

You are feeling lonely. Release the belief that is keeping you from asking for help and be ready to receive. True sharing goes both ways, and this does not make you vulnerable or weak in the eyes of others. You are only human!

**If you see a flock of egrets**
A community, charitable organisation or family are spheres in which you can invest your energy to develop your sense of mutual aid and togetherness.

**If you see an egret on the back of a cow**
It would be useful to speak to someone to get sound advice, because sometimes it is good to seek an outside opinion. Don't hesitate to ask a person you trust for insight, as it could open your mind up to new possibilities on an issue you're facing.

## BUILDING TOGETHER

Cathy needed to release the burden she was inflicting on herself by wanting to manage everything alone since her break-up. During a soul reading the egret came to her as her totem animal and talked about her ability to coordinate the skills of other people in the service of a common cause. By underlining this strength the egret reminded Cathy that we can never build anything alone. Reassuring Cathy on her capacity to remain independent in her relationships with others, the egret brought her greater self-kindness as well as the broader view she needed.

# Elephant

Element: **earth**

Season: **summer**

Keywords: **truth, earth guardian, revelations**

Elephants are guardians of the earth, and they carry that energy. Their ability to perceive seismic waves through the soles of their feet connects them to the deeps. Cheating is pointless with the elephant: the truth will come out, the masks will come off and people who play a role will be revealed to themselves. It is time to be truthful with yourself. The elephant and its resonance are here to help you heal through vibes of love. If a part of you is hidden away, it might be time to reveal it: the elephant knows who you really are!

## MESSAGES

If you act like a chameleon to please others you will end up losing yourself. This attitude comes into being when you are strongly lacking in self-confidence and adapt to others, but over time this adaptation mechanism turns into an automatic reflex and it becomes difficult to dig out your true personality. The elephant has come to help you see yourself for who you truly are, and to stop you from being afraid to show that face to the world.

### Relationships

*If you are in a relationship*: a relationship needs a bedrock of trust, and some revelations enable two people to start over on a strong

# E

basis. Trying to show yourself in the best possible light will get you nowhere. Love yourself as you are, and don't be afraid of being authentic with your partner.

*If you are single*: the elephant is telling you that you can't please everyone. Start by pleasing yourself and stop trying to adapt all the time, because that is how you will attract the right people.

## Work

Whatever your area of work you need time to adapt and find your place in a company or with the people you mix with. Knowing how to stay true to yourself despite a need to please is a quality that will enable you to live openly and be recognised for who you are.

## Family

To reveal yourself as you are you need to have a good understanding of who you are. It's important to take time to look back on your history, seek out elders who are still here and ask them questions, so you can identify the family memories you may have inherited. It is also an opportunity to discover any talents your ancestors may have had.

## Health

If you are a smoker, cigarettes have an effect on you similar to a smoke screen behind which you hide from the world. Whatever your addiction, it is keeping you away from your innermost self. The elephant will help you free yourself from your addictions and stand firm in your quest to attain a better state of well-being.

## SPECIAL MESSAGES

### If you see an elephant

There is something you don't realise about yourself. You are most probably going to make an interesting discovery about your ancestors and the gifts they passed down to you, and this discovery will change your reality.

**If you dream of an elephant**

A particular part of you wants to exist. How can you be yourself in all circumstances? Ask yourself, 'Am I the same person everywhere and with everyone?' If you feel you have a tendency to adapt to others too much, ask the elephant for help.

## AN ALLY FOR LIFE

Eve still vividly recalls her encounter with an elephant when she was a child: 'I was five years old, and my family and I had gone to visit a circus and menagerie. When we were there I saw an elephant in an enclosure with a block of wood tied to one of its legs. I wanted to free it, so I slipped under the fence. My parents and the staff were worried and called to me to come back. I heard them, but I still went up to the elephant. I touched its trunk and gave it a kiss. The elephant was very gentle with me. I knew I had to go back, and at in that instant it touched me delicately with its trunk. It was probably telling me that I couldn't stay, that I had to return to my parents. When I think back to that amazing moment I can see the look in its eyes and I can smell its scent.'

At the tender age of five, Eve innocently went over to see an elephant and felt the purity of its intentions. The elephant became her ally for life and its energy continues to guide her on her path.

# Ewe

Element: **earth**
Season: **spring**
Keywords: **individuality, group energy, conditioning**

Ewes have a tendency to let themselves be carried by the energy of the flock because they know they can rest in that energy. This is a great quality but also a fault, as their lack of distinctiveness reveals a fragility and a difficulty living in alignment with who they are individually. Ewes are destined to remain in the group to escape marauding wolves. The ewe speaks to you about your difficulty in moving away from the patterns of your education and culture even though they limit you. You feel that if you dared to be different it would be dangerous for the social or moral order.

## MESSAGES

Don't be afraid to be yourself and displease, and then don't expect others to validate your difference. Rather, become the head ewe of the flock, the one who takes everyone down a fresh path. Have no fear of getting lost beyond your boundaries, for you will soon invent new ones that look like you and work better for you. In doing so you will inspire others, who will be able to choose to live as they wish to.

### Relationships

*If you are in a relationship*: every relationship is different, so it is pointless to compare yourself with others. Follow your heart. The important thing is to feel respected and loved; everything else is just conventions and formalities. Don't let social norms influence your relationship!

*If you are single*: loneliness can be a scary feeling, but it would be a mistake to try to find someone at all costs to fill the void. Solitude could even be a fulfilling path if you changed your point of view on it and stopped trying to fit into a particular mould. Living alone isn't necessarily a failure: it can also be a choice, and who knows? Perhaps love will come into your life when you least expect it to.

## Work

Your workplace could be compared with a flock of sheep managed by shepherds. Raising awareness means refusing to let others lose their own light. Whether you're a sheep or a shepherd doesn't matter, because the important thing is to stay true to your opinions and help others express their own.

## Family

A black sheep is one who does nothing like everyone else, who often disappoints and is criticised because they disturb, yet someone who defies the rules enables their clan to heal from limiting patterns and achieve the unspoken dreams of their ancestors. If you feel this is relevant to you, know that your place is very important and that you can be proud of yourself. Don't minimise the impact of your role within your family.

## Health

The problem with ewes is that they don't always think enough for themselves. Some ways or influences can be positive, but others can be dangerous for your health. Avoid brutal or radical changes in diet and listen to your body. If you smoke, could it just be to give you a feeling of belonging?

# E

### If you see a ewe alone

You are on the right track to free yourself from aspects of your conditioning. Keep sorting through what truly matters to you so you can maintain a framework in your life, and be more flexible with the rest. Nothing is immutable; do your best to follow your personal values.

### If you see a flock of ewes

You are plagued by self-doubt and still place too much weight on what others may think. Inspire others instead of going with the flow. Become your own leader and you will see that everything will happen for the best.

# Falcon

Element: **air**
Season: **winter**
Keywords: **intuition, inner voice, choices**

Falcons have the ability to hover in flight to take the time to evaluate a situation before diving on their prey. The falcon's flight invites you to listen to your inner voice, the one that knows whether you are taking the right path and making the right decision. Falcons are undisputed masters of intuition and rapid action. Intuition is a furtive thing: you need to learn to catch it as it flies past and trust in yourself in the present moment so you can serenely make your way forward.

## MESSAGES

Trust in yourself, because a spontaneous choice is often the right one. The falcon wants to teach you to catch the furtive message of your soul just before your mind grabs hold of the situation and complicates everything.

### Relationships

*If you are in a relationship*: intuition is what guided you both to find each other. The falcon knows that your relationship is a meeting of souls, even if you sometimes still doubt it. Those doubts are healthy, so don't try to sidestep them. Just be sure that you have something to experience together.

*If you are single*: when you stop trying to control your mind you make room for fleeting but intense feelings that may be qualified as calls of the soul. If your thoughts fly towards a particular person then follow your heart without hesitation!

## Work

Sometimes you can sense that an email is on its way before it hits your inbox. That intuitive part of you can make a place for itself in your work life. There is no need to change everything, but you can learn to surf on the waves of your intuition and see the impact this can have on your work.

## Family

You are all connected in your family, and you instinctively know if someone is going through a difficult time. You may feel some kind of malaise without understanding the reason for it and then learn that someone in your inner circle isn't well. Use this link to communicate your love for the people around you.

## Health

You may sometimes feel that something is not well in your body but you don't give yourself permission to hear it until the problem stands out so badly that it can no longer be denied. Instead of neglecting the signs issued by your body, take them into account. This won't make you weak or self-centred; on the contrary, it is the way of good health, of an alliance between body and mind.

## SPECIAL MESSAGES

### If you see a falcon sitting still

Your body needs to be well maintained and cared for. If you have taken a raincheck on a medical appointment, book it again. Don't wait for the situation to deteriorate before taking action.

## If you see a falcon hovering in flight

An intuition has just hit you, or it will come to you in the course of the day. Instead of allowing it to get lost in doubts fabricated by your mind, give that intuition a choice spot in your heart away from your thoughts.

## If you see a falcon diving on its prey

You will soon be presented with a choice. Listen to your inner voice.

# Firefly

Element: **air**

Season: **summer**

Keywords: **poetry, inner light, dreams**

Fireflies symbolise the poetic beauty of the night and light in the dark. As a power animal, the firefly enlightens the soul on the beauty of life and points it towards resilience. Whatever path it may have taken, your soul can heal and access the happiness it deserves. The firefly speaks of childhood wounds and the dreams you let fall to the side of the road.

## MESSAGE

Your ability to heal never left you: it is here, and your inner light is showing you the way. Life is a poem that you must write. Leave your painful experiences behind you to let your inner light shine, because in that light there are sleeping childhood dreams.

# Flamingo

Element: **water**
Season: **autumn**
Keywords: **love, energy, direction**

This gorgeous pink bird has a habit of standing on one leg to save energy and conserve heat. The flamingo as a power animal invites you to direct your attention towards what truly nourishes you and makes you shine. The flamingo's heart beats for love in all its forms, and urges you to bring that energy into your heart.

## MESSAGES

Love is an inexhaustible source of energy and heat. When you find yourself in a cold atmosphere or an environment that is poor in love you can connect with the energy of the flamingo to stay on course. Love exists in many different forms, and you are in a constant relationship with this universal frequency. The flamingo invites you to see how you can bring more love into your life.

# F

# Fly

Element: **fire**
Season: **summer**
Keywords: **letting go, transformation, movement**

Flies are generally considered to be pests, invasive nuisances that propagate everywhere, but they are really just opportunists looking for food and warmth. When you make an effort to look beyond your distaste you can open yourself to the fly's message. Flies carry an energy of rapid transformation as well as a sense of urgency, as though there was something that needs to be understood right now. There is no time to look back: you are being called to let go.

## MESSAGES

The fly invites you to set yourself in motion. You may have fallen asleep in your comfort zone, and the fly wants to bring new energy into an aspect of your life that you have set aside. It may be time to think about going out, finding your way back to the gym, spending time with people, embarking on a new project or changing something that no longer works for you. You are being called to get a move on!

### Relationships

*If you are in a relationship*: a good, informal discussion would help you and your partner communicate and start a healthy conversation within your relationship. Don't hesitate to speak from the heart so you can begin anew on more solid foundations.

*If you are single*: change your habits to discover different places where you can easily meet people.

## Work

Is something not working for you? By recognising and affirming what is blocking you, you will be able to take things forward. Start by admitting what is running interference with you so that you can come up with solutions. The universe will hear your request.

## Family

Family relationships can sometimes be harmful, and you feel conflicting needs inside you. On the one hand you want to enjoy the presence of your loved ones, but on the other you need some time alone with yourself. Listen to your needs and give yourself permission to do things differently, otherwise you will exhaust your energy.

## Health

Beware of excesses! It is important for you to eat healthy foods, and you may need to rebalance your nutritional intake. If you feel the need to go on a diet you should be assisted by a specialist.

## SPECIAL MESSAGES

### If a fly is sticking to you like glue and following you everywhere
You need to let go of a situation that is preventing you from finding fulfilment.

### If you have a great many flies in your house
It is time to sort through your thoughts for greater clarity. Take time to consider what you have experienced over the past month and determine your needs for the one to come. Depending on the area of

your life in which you have questions, refer to the theme-related information to obtain a message from the fly.

### If flies have laid eggs in your kitchen
You absolutely need to regularly cleanse your energy and cannot wait until you've reached the lowest low to take action. It is by taking daily care of that energy that you will feel full of vitality.

### If you see flies on the decomposing body of a dead animal
Change is called for in your life. If you listen to your heart you already know that it is time to move on to something else.

## A RELENTLESS FLY

This story was shared by Manon: 'After quite a few trainings in animal communication and personal development I began to discern the present moment, even if I wasn't then able to experience it. I noticed that for the past two weeks a fly had been following me around everywhere in my paramedical office, in the relaxation room and the waiting room. It had clearly come to tell me to let go!

'After trying in vain to make that fly go away I started to question what I was unsuccessfully trying to control. I came to the realisation that being self-employed no longer worked for me. I accepted that, and I informed my patients. A young man asked to come and train with me, and he took over my practice. Once I was ready to listen to what the fly was trying to tell me everything began to flow.'

# Fox

Element: **fire**
Season: **autumn**
Keywords: **play, vigour, shyness, rejection**

Foxes have been rejected and hunted for a long time. For this reason, out of shyness and fear of that rejection they won't appear to just anyone, yet they are jokers with a captivating, vigorous energy that is directed at play. When foxes feel secure they reveal their true, tender, endearing personalities.

## MESSAGES

The fox has come to make you work on your fear of rejection. Out of fear of being negatively judged you hide away your true personality, and it is only in the presence of trusted loved ones that you manage to be yourself and reveal your cheerful and playful nature. If you try to set aside your fears and go towards others you don't know you might meet some wonderful people.

### Relationships
*If you are in a relationship*: your rejection wound sometimes leads you to act out of fear of your partner's reaction. Humour is the best way to get your message across in a friendly atmosphere. Your partner loves that mischievous aspect of your personality.

*If you are single*: it is time to dive into the unknown and reveal yourself as you truly are. Your personality traits are assets filled with charm that should never be hidden out of fear of not being liked. Be yourself so you can meet someone who truly understands you.

### Work

Work doesn't have to rhyme with boredom. If you could bring a touch of folly to your job, what would you do? Lightening up the atmosphere is a good way to bond with your co-workers, so make good use of your charm and don't be afraid of not being liked. Mindsets have changed!

### Family

You're the joker and entertainer in your family, a role that can sometimes irritate you because you feel you aren't taken seriously, but this is only a reflection of your wound of rejection. Know that without you, the atmosphere would be rather sad. Keep your jokiness alive whatever you do; your best asset is keeping your family united.

### Health

Your energy and good humour ensure your good health. You are in great shape! Heartburn and digestive disorders are the main issues that can affect you when you feel you are in a hostile environment. In such cases, your inner fire turns against you.

## SPECIAL MESSAGES

### If you see a fox

It is time to break free from your shyness. Don't be afraid to go towards others and bond with new people. Rejection is no longer an issue, and you are being called to shine out your joyful personality.

### If you see a fox that has been run over by a car

You still vibe with the energy of rejection and are afraid of others. As long as you remain unaware of this you will keep attracting situations of rejection, which is a great pity because in doing so you prevent yourself from seeing things as they truly are.

## A SAVING ENCOUNTER

Sandra came upon a dead fox on the side of the road as she was leaving for a date with her new boyfriend. Intrigued by this encounter, she asked me what it meant: her family was actually rejecting her new relationship. A year later that rejection had come to the point where she felt as though she herself was being snubbed by the people she loved.

After listening to what they had to say she finally understood that, intoxicated by her feelings for this man, she hadn't seen him as he truly was and her family had only been trying to protect her. She decided to break up with her boyfriend, and the love lavished on her by her family in the wake of that decision helped her heal her rejection wound.

# Frog

Element: **water**
Season: **spring**
Keywords: **transformation, ordeals, inner world**

Frogs live through different stages of transformation before they reach adulthood. At each of these stages they undergo many ordeals and have slim chances of survival, yet they get there in the end! Frogs are warriors, and they want to see their metamorphoses through so they can enjoy life singing in a pond. The frog appears to give you the self-confidence you need to set your course towards your dreams whatever may happen.

## MESSAGES

Self-development isn't an activity to engage in as a Sunday hobby: it is a lengthy process of working on yourself to grow and evolve. Like frogs, you will have to visit your wounds and go through painful times to take ownership of your shadow parts before you can see the light, but with each transformation your soul will reveal itself a little more and guide your spirit towards what it holds most sacred.

### Relationships

*If you are in a relationship*: a relationship has a lot to do with transformation. From the moment you meet until you have an established life together there are many stages involving inner questioning and doubts. If you want to have a chance of a peaceful life in your pond you need to take risks and make your way forward, even if that means making a mistake and having to start all over again.

*If you are single*: you are no longer the person you used to be. Time has made you grow and life may have given you a few knocks. Like a frog, you have lived through many challenges. The frog urges you not to lose your direction. You are on your path, and happiness is waiting for you at the end of the road. Don't despair!

## Work

A career is far from a straight path, as it can involve mountains and cliffs, stops and hollows, yet you will get where you are meant to be. Consider these stages as being essential to the building of your path and the development of your deep personality.

## Family

Together, we are stronger. Like a frog, when you find yourself as potential prey you know that being part of a group increases your chances of survival. Reconnect with this spirit of solidarity within your clan in order not to feel lonely. If you have no family you can invest your energy in a society or charitable organisation to feel stronger.

## Health

Your body and cells react to your thoughts and emotions. Reflect on the frog's process of transformation and feel how your body has that same capacity for regeneration. Trust in your body, cherishing it for what it allows you to do. If it is sick, send it all your love to help it heal more quickly.

## SPECIAL MESSAGES

### If you find a frog in your garden

Don't forget your goal, because you will achieve it. Keep dreaming and finding new projects for yourself, as that is what motivates you.

### If you find a frog in your home
You have known many ordeals and have great mental strength. Spend time reflecting on how far you've come and recognise your adaptability. You can go where you like and are capable of many things.

### If you find a clutch of frog eggs
A project or new dream is about to blossom. Embrace it like a gift and nurture it, for it will lead you to exploring new territory.

### If you see tadpoles
Competition is cut-throat, and you have to elbow your way through to make a place for yourself. Rather than panicking, have faith in your inner strength to get yourself out of this tight spot.

### If you see lots of baby frogs
Your numerous ideas will bring to life many projects that you can choose to see through to the end or not. You will naturally select the ones to carry forward depending on your priorities.

### If you hear frogs singing
Keep your motivation intact, for you will soon achieve your goal.

# Giraffe

Element: **spirit**
Season: **summer**
Keywords: **dreams, art, creation**

With their incredibly long necks, giraffes seem to reach beyond the clouds. Their spirit energy makes them guardians of sky spirits, and giraffes establish a link between these spirits and our earthly world. They can give the impression of having their minds on other things and even of being a little absent-minded, but make no mistake: they are well grounded and know their mission. The giraffe is an ally for dreamers, scatterbrained people and those who have their heads in the clouds but who actually travel into subtle realms.

## MESSAGE

For the giraffe, dreaming means touching with your heart what you will create. This power animal invites you to let yourself be cradled by your imagination, for it is often in that dimension that spirits will inspire you with ideas, seeds to grow within you. Then, with its earthly grounding, the giraffe will help you materialise what you see in your dreams. Make what is invisible, visible: that is the mission entrusted to you by the giraffe.

# Goat, billy
## (and ibex)

Element: **earth**
Season: **summer**
Keywords: **protection, sacrifices, obstacles**

Billy goats are a force of nature, go-getters that never hesitate for a second when it comes to defending their herds. These big-hearted protectors can sometimes go to the extent of sacrificing themselves to keep face, for they hate to lose. The billy goat will appear to you if you need to learn to be more flexible, because your hard-headedness sometimes makes you build walls where there are no barriers.

## MESSAGES

The universe sets onto your path what you need to experience, and billy goats are a prime example of this. When you behave like a conqueror then life will bring you adversaries and obstacles to overcome. However, when you move forward without this combative energy then barriers melt away and you enter into a dimension of peace. What do you choose to experience? Drop your weapons, and you will see that you are not in danger.

### Relationships

*If you are in a relationship*: the billy goat invites you to not sacrifice yourself for others. Your protective side can sometimes be too invasive and you do too much, when all that is expected of you is to just be there for your partner.

*If you are single*: you are an endearing person but you can sometimes be too direct. Take things down a notch to soften your words and give the person in front of you more room so they can express their point of view. Keep an open mind!

## Work

You certainly see things through once you've started, but at what price? Why don't you take a break once in a while, catch your breath and look at what you have already accomplished? You will see that breaks are a way of conserving your strength.

## Family

Family is a sensitive topic for you, one that can turn into a fight. You proudly defend your tribe and let no one step on your toes. This is very much to your credit and you are driven by your big heart, but take care to protect yourself. It is sometimes wiser to avoid riding into battle altogether.

## Health

You have a lot of energy, but anger and anxiety can deplete your reserves and leave you having no strength left at all. Be bold, ask for help, allow yourself some rest and delegate certain tasks, and you will again attain a measure of peace.

## SPECIAL MESSAGES

### If you dream of a billy goat

The billy goat is coming to warn you of an impending conflict. Ideally, don't overreact to the offensive but instead think before deciding what to do.

### If you see a billy goat

Take care not to be in constant action. Rushing headlong into a situation won't help you see things any more clearly.

# Goat, nanny

Element: **earth**
Season: **winter**
Keywords: **agility, character, stubbornness**

Nanny goats are agile creatures that are able to jump from rock to rock to reach their food. They know how to make good use of their intelligence to get what they want, but behind their docile appearance lies a very strong character. Nanny goats do just as they please and can be quite stubborn. This power animal will appear to you if you are in need of tempering your momentum and learning to collaborate with others. You will go faster alone but further together.

## MESSAGES

You are very good at unearthing unusual finds and valuable ideas but you can sometimes be reluctant to work with others. The nanny goat has come to remove your blinders to help you be willing to collaborate. You will go much further if you lean on the skills of others. Surround yourself with the right people so you can attain your goal.

### Relationships

*If you are in a relationship*: you forget to count on your partner and sometimes act as though you are single. Don't forget to take your partner's opinion into account before making choices.

*If you are single*: you have been going it alone for a long time, so the day you meet someone you will have to adapt. Are you ready to alter your habits? Relationships are about making concessions.

## Work

Don't rush on ahead without first considering the atmosphere around you and your colleagues' motivation. If there are many of you to carry a project it will necessarily have more weight. Of course, you will lose the benefit of having taken it forward alone, but it will have had the advantage of a more powerful and durable momentum.

## Family

Nanny goats know how to surround themselves with others, because they need the strength of the herd to feel safe. Don't isolate yourself from the people you love when you're not doing well. On the contrary, ask your friends or family for help.

## Health

You are focused on your activities to the point of forgetting your body's needs, and have a tendency to overstep your limits. Lift your foot from the pedal once in a while and take a break, because then you will go further.

## SPECIAL MESSAGES

### If you see a nanny goat

Your idea is interesting but needs to be matured with the help of others. Share this idea with your loved ones to enrich your project.

### If you dream of a nanny goat

Your attitude is too exclusive, and it is detrimental to your action within the group. You are being invited to be more collaborative and will be rewarded for your efforts to share.

# Goldfinch

Element: **air**

Season: **summer**

Keywords: **appearances, judgement, benevolence**

Goldfinches are connected with the fragility of ecosystems. Threatened by poaching, these little birds still know how to take good advantage of a situation and can even find food on thistle stalks. Even the spikiest plant has some worth. The goldfinch teaches you not to judge at first glance, and to be kind to other people and try to get to know them better.

## MESSAGE

Take time to think before judging someone. Don't rely on a single meeting or moment, for that first impression isn't representative of who that person is. It is also sometimes a good idea to review an old judgement and allow yourself to reconsider the situation or person involved.

# Goldfish

Element: **fire**

Season: **summer**

Keywords: **present moment, joy, discovery**

Goldfish don't have long-term memories, which forces them to live in the present moment. You might find this sad, yet how much time do you lose in reliving or imagining scenarios that will never happen? With the goldfish, celebration and joy happen right now! This power animal's energy sparkles like a child enraptured by something new. With each day bringing novelty, the goldfish has no need to dream about a different time or space as it creates everything in the here and now.

## MESSAGE

Don't waste your time imagining possible scenarios, as there is very little chance of them unfolding in the way you project. Life is short, and the present moment is filled with magic. The goldfish invites you to enjoy each moment with the eyes of a child. If you focus on the here and now, you will be better able to build the future.

G

# Goose

Element: **air**
Season: **summer**
Keywords: **trust, cohesion, groups**

Geese imprint on the first being they see when they hatch, and that being becomes their figure of attachment. If they imprint on a human being they will give that person their immediate trust, so some tamers use this process to create a bond with them. Geese live in flocks, and during migration they form a V shape to support each other during flight. The goose will appear to you if you need to find new trust in human relationships.

## MESSAGES

Your optimistic nature makes you believe in humanity even if you may on occasion have been disappointed by people who betrayed your trust. The goose has come to remind you that your first impression is often correct. When you meet someone you are able to feel whether they are dependable or not, and you are invited to reconnect with this instinct.

### Relationships

*If you are in a relationship*: trust is the foundation of a stable and durable relationship. Set aside the bad experiences of your past to build projects together serenely and without ulterior motives.

*If you are single*: love is a wonderful feeling. No matter how many failed romantic relationships you may have experienced, your heart is always able to love. Know that it is also possible for you to make a fresh start despite the events in your past.

## Work

You need a positive environment to be able to give your work your best. A cohesive team is just as important to you as your own job.

## Family

Your family is your anchor, and your personal fulfilment is tied to the love you get from the people around you. However, to really feel good you need your loved ones to be happy.

## Health

The well-being of your loved ones can have an impact on your happiness. If a person you love is going through an ordeal you will feel greatly impacted due to your empathy for them. The goose advises you to remember to also take care of yourself when you give someone moral support or any other form of help.

## SPECIAL MESSAGES

### If you see a goose

You need to recover your trust in your relationships with others. Believe in your instinct and intuition to maintain authentic ties with people.

### If you see wild geese

The strength of the flock invites you to rethink your role within your family, work and hobbies. Where can you find this cohesion and mutual aid?

# Grasshopper

Element: **air**

Season: **spring**

Keywords: **lightness, steps forward, comfort zone**

Grasshoppers are insects with an ability to quickly jump out of a precarious spot to explore new places. The grasshopper hops merrily from one comfort zone to another and always moves forwards with joy.

## MESSAGES

The grasshopper has come to reassure you that life is good, and you need to be bold and hop out of your personal domain to go on an exploration of life. What would you like to explore? Think about it, and notice the joy that idea brings you.

### Relationships

*If you are in a relationship*: plan for a little get-away together, even just for a weekend, in an unusual place. It will bring you closer.

*If you are single*: enjoy life and its pleasures. Hop from one branch to the next, and appreciate trips to different places and change.

### Work

Give yourself some breathing space, and have fun in your work. You run the risk of suffocating if you don't take things with a lighter heart. Let your joyful nature express itself.

## Family

Places belonging to a family for generations can be a burden. The grasshopper invites you not to invest too much energy in them, otherwise you might lose your cheerfulness.

## Health

You need your life to be as light and joyful as possible so you can feel in shape. Avoid too much stress and too many frustrations so you remain in a good mood.

## SPECIAL MESSAGES

**If you see a grasshopper**
Life is good, so smile!

**If a grasshopper lands on you**
Why don't you turn off the stress? You'll see if you do that you feel much better afterwards.

**If you find a grasshopper in your house**
You are going to experience a lot of family joy, so appreciate it.

**If you find a grasshopper in your car**
You need an outing or trip somewhere to clear your head.

# Greenfinch

Element: **air**
Season: **spring**
Keywords: **hope, lightness, happiness**

With their green feathers dipped in bright yellow, greenfinches bear a message of hope. When the greenfinch appears in your life it is a sign that you have rather lost faith in your lucky star. This little bird's heart knows that the sun always comes back after the rain.

## MESSAGE

The greenfinch comes to project rays of sunlight into your life. Spring always comes back to blossom after the end of winter, fields turn green again and you yearn to reconnect with hope for a lighter and happier life. Keep faith, for the greenfinch has come to bring you what you were missing: that ray of hope you need so you can believe. Anything is possible!

# Green shield bug

Element: **earth**
Season: **spring**
Keywords: **defence, protection, self-confidence**

Green shield bugs are harmless to humans; they just emit a disgusting smell when they are disturbed or crushed. Despite their small size their defence mechanism is very efficient, and the green shield bug comes to remind you that size isn't everything. When you feel threatened you mustn't doubt your ability to scare off those who want to pick a fight. Having confidence in your potential can change a situation.

## MESSAGES

Have you ever felt disconcerted by aggressive behaviour or gratuitous viciousness? The green shield bug comes to remind you that even if you want to vibe in harmony with others, it is perfectly natural to protect yourself from gratuitous attacks. Some people, far from being awakened, only live in duality. You are invited to activate your personal defence system to scare off such people, who will feel that your protective barrier is well entrenched.

### Relationships

*If you are in a relationship*: jealousy is generally a source of tension in a relationship but in small doses it can show your partner that you care for them, like a guardrail against potential rivals.

*If you are single*: your defence system has often helped you exit sticky situations in the past. Keep it intact, but try to modulate its strength depending on the situation. Otherwise you might put off potential suitors.

## Work

Competition is a useful thing you need to be able to stand out from the crowd and show what you can do. Competition can even on occasion be the way to showcase the quality of your work. Don't be afraid of others; trust in your potential!

## Family

You have known rivalry in your family circle in the past, and it is sometimes still difficult for you to find your place. Don't remain in power struggles. Sibling rivalry is natural throughout the animal kingdom, as a way of learning to activate someone's defence system. Look at how it has strengthened your own character.

## Health

Fear of others can have an effect on your kidneys, so drink a lot of water and take stock of your anxiety triggers. Contrarily, if you are comfortable with others the green shield bug may be inviting you to temper your excessive yang or masculine energy with greater gentleness.

## SPECIAL MESSAGES

### If you find a green shield bug in your house
There is an issue of jealously or rivalry in your family circle. Look in that direction and try to see your loved ones as allies.

### If you find a green shield bug on you
Your energy field is well balanced and you have an efficient protection system. Congratulations: you have found a happy medium!

## If you are invaded by green shield bugs

It is time to assess your need for protection. Learn to create a protective bubble around you to preserve your energy.

## If you find a dead green shield bug

A conflicting situation will end when you become aware of its usefulness. In other words, that conflict holds teachings for you.

# Groundhog

Element: **earth**

Season: **winter**

Keywords: **solidarity, social life, interpersonal skills**

Groundhogs have very rich social lives. Their energy is directed towards solidarity, and they make sure that the tribe is governed by harmony. The groundhog is close to people who have a gift for human relations, who know how to listen and are good company. This power animal will appear to help you if you have underestimated your interpersonal skills and should use them more often in your daily life.

## MESSAGES

You are very good at taking care of others, anticipating their needs and working for the well-being of everyone you meet. You have a place to take in helping others. If you already have, the groundhog encourages you to take on even more responsibilities in your current position, especially in areas of administration or management. To fully invest your energy you need to know that your efforts will mean something and will respect human values. When you feel truly useful nothing can stop you!

### Relationships

*If you are in a relationship*: your life with your partner is very important to you. Communication between the two of you is excellent, which means it is possible for you to make your relationship last a long time.

Keep using your interpersonal skills to enhance communication between you even further.

*If you are single*: it is sometimes easier for you to help others find a partner than it is for you to identify the right person for yourself, yet you are well familiar with the wa y love operates and have an eye for rare jewels. Give yourself permission to find one for yourself!

## Work

You have a disconcerting ability to resolve interpersonal problems and analyse people's needs, which would make you an excellent manager. If your job is related in some way to helping others then you are in the right place. If you work in a different field, see how you can use your capacities in your work.

## Family

If there are conflicts or old quarrels in your family, use your mediation talents to smooth out communication between people. You know how to maintain a good entente within your clan.

## Health

You have very positive energy and people come to you easily. You do need to feel useful to be in good physical form, because you draw strength from that. Take care, however, because if you spend all your energy on others you won't have any left for yourself.

## SPECIAL MESSAGES

### If you see a groundhog
Your role in society needs to evolve as you have skills that are waiting to be put at the service of others. You will derive great joy and pleasure in finding fulfilment in areas to do with human relations and mutual aid.

### If you dream of groundhogs
Let your desire to be useful reveal the way ahead to you.

# Hedgehog

Element: **earth**

Season: **autumn**

Keywords: **kindness, energy boundaries, protection**

Hedgehogs are full of love and tenderness. Their only weapon of defence is to curl up into a tight ball, for their spines dissuade potential predators. The hedgehog will appear to you if you are in need of extending your bubble of protection to recover your personal space. Just because you are an empathetic person does not mean you need to be willing to accept everything from others, and certainly not their negative energy! Learning to defend yourself on an energy level can involve imagining that you are protected by spines defending you on an invisible level. It can also involve setting an intention to protect the beautiful energy that lives inside you.

## MESSAGES

You are a kind person and people often tell you so, but people also often take advantage of you because you never say 'No.' This 'No' has to be established on an energy level first. Setting boundaries will not in any way modify your generous nature: on the contrary, you will preserve that nature for people who really deserve it. Visualise your bubble, the one you're surrounded by, and imagine adding spines to it as though you are a hedgehog and you'll see that many people who would take advantage of you will naturally stay away. Next, learn how to say 'No!'

## Relationships

*If you are in a relationship*: your kindness and generous nature lead you to want to please your partner, but you don't always express your own needs enough and then you feel misunderstood. You deserve to be paid attention to as well. This reciprocity will enable you to be happy to make your partner happy.

*If you are single*: as with the hedgehog your likeable nature immediately attracts many friends, but do you really want to only be a friend? Don't cultivate a role that could result in sadness for you and be clear about your intentions.

## Work

Some people come to draw inspiration from you and then appropriate your ideas. The hedgehog has come to help you protect yourself from being taken advantage of. Visualise a protective bubble around you to keep away opportunists.

## Family

Your family are kind, generous people and you have inherited these traits. You can be proud of this heritage but must still be like the hedgehog, knowing how to preserve what matters to you and sort through your relationships.

## Health

Your tendency to accept a lot from people can sometimes turn you into an emotional sponge, which is why it's essential for you to set personal and energy boundaries. Keep your generosity for people who won't take advantage of it and stay away from energy vampires.

## SPECIAL MESSAGES

### If you have a hedgehog in your garden

Consider your needs in your personal life and within your family. Don't go beyond what you can give, and dare to ask for help so you can have some breathing space. You deserve to be taken care of in the same way that you take care of others.

### If you come across a hedgehog
Remember that your limits take effect on an energy level before anything else. Don't let a bad mood or negative thinking cripple your benevolence.

### If you see a hedgehog that has been run over by a car
Know how to set your boundaries, in love and in friendship. You have the right not to systematically agree with your interlocutor, as constant agreement does no one any favours. Be bold and frank in your relationships. You have enough benevolence in you to get your message across, and you will gain in authenticity.

# Hen

Element: **earth**
Season: **winter**
Keywords: **hunger, food, scarcity**

Hens are connected with the nurturing and maternal dimension of the earth. They teach you that if you take care of the earth it will give you material and spiritual food. The hen comes to heal your fear of scarcity and your memories of famine and war. This power animal will bring security to you if you need to feel supported.

## MESSAGES

You may be someone who needs to store up on food, because without knowing why you worry about not having enough. Hunger can maybe even make you aggressive, and the hen wants to help you release that fear. Abundance is everywhere, and earthly as well as spiritual foods are within reach if you release ancestral memories related to hunger.

### Relationships
*If you are in a relationship*: fear of scarcity can make you rely on your partner for financial, material or emotional support. That fear is polluting your relationship, so try to recover your independence so you can enjoy a more harmonious love.

*If you are single*: feelings of scarcity and fear go against true encounters. If you feel concerned by memories of this sort, release them now so you can avoid meeting someone who resonates with the same issues.

You may have already in the past experienced a relationship where you depended on your partner. It is time to release that.

### Work

Your work can bring abundance to your door if you release your fear of scarcity. Don't worry, as you have the capacity to support your family. The hen will help you move forward on your way to freedom.

### Family

Working to release issues of scarcity and hunger could enable you to feel more secure, or at least less anxious, about the question of abundance in your life. What belongs in the past needs to be accepted in order for it to stop manifesting in your today.

### Health

A feeling of inner insecurity can lead you to excesses, especially in relation to food or emotions. Your body needs to understand that it has no need to store things up, because you want for nothing. Your fear is actually something you inherited from your family.

## SPECIAL MESSAGES

### If you feel an urge to raise hens

You have managed to turn your fear of scarcity into an asset to support your family. You are invited to become aware of the mechanisms at work inside you, as the hen is bringing you a feeling of security.

### If you have chicks

Family ties are at the root of your anxiety and need to protect your loved ones and make sure they are provided for. This is a positive quality, but it should not impact your happiness with your family. Don't worry: you can do it!

**If you see a hen**

Abundance is first and foremost in your heart. Feel how you are free from want and how you have access to spiritual nourishment.

**If one of your hens is eaten by a fox or a stone marten**

Family memories are expressing themselves in connection with the death of a loved one or a feeling of scarcity associated with brutal loss. This could be about you or a member of your family. To recover a feeling of inner security it is time to become aware of any compensation mechanisms you may have established.

# H

# Heron

Element: **air**
Season: **spring**
Keywords: **grace, feminine principle, flow**

Herons live near rivers and lakes. These big, beautiful birds support the feminine principle of water and help improve the flow of emotions. Their lightness and grace take this yin energy, indispensable to embracing the movements of life, into the air. With the heron, everything is calm and love flows in its vital fluid. Herons have a cold energy, observing shifts in the water and moving towards areas where they can recharge.

## MESSAGES

Life is like a river, running its course until it reaches the sea or the ocean. The heron invites you to take a break once in a while to consider the course of your life and recharge. Check your energy points to allow the day's emotions to flow through you.

### Relationships

*If you are in a relationship*: the feminine principle brings harmony to your relationship, because you let yourself be guided by your life experiences. Love is at the heart of your story and is an essential aspect of your mutual revitalisation.

*If you are single*: you know exactly how to renew your energy and a romantic relationship is a central point of this renewal, but if your relationship isn't a source of fulfilment for you then you'd prefer to take flight to find another source.

## Work

You fly over obstacles with lightness and grace and let negative energy slip by, and when a situation becomes complicated you know how to recharge your batteries. For you, work is like a rock in the middle of a stream: when your way is blocked by a large obstacle you prefer to go around it.

## Family

When faced with a storm you know how to rise above the situation until the waters become less turbulent. In this way you manage your energy well and continue to be a source of peace for the people around you.

## Health

Your vital fluid is calm, peaceful and cold. You may be sensitive to changes in temperature and mood when you don't take sufficient time to re-energise. If you allow yourself these necessary breaks your feminine principle will enable you to follow the flow for a long time.

## SPECIAL MESSAGES

### If you see a heron on a riverbank

Well done: you know how to find ways to ground yourself and recharge your batteries. Your energy is in excellent shape thanks to the time you give yourself to renew it.

### If you see a heron near a lake

Your inner water is a little stagnant. Take care not to accumulate too much stress or your vitality and health will bear the consequences. Take time to recharge on a regular basis.

### If you see a heron take flight

When a situation becomes too heavy, rise above it to keep a cool head. By allowing yourself the time you need to think about it you will act for the best. Don't be impulsive.

### If you see a heron perched on a branch

It seems that a source that enables you to recharge may have run dry. Whether it is a family member, animal, place or something else, try to find other sources of calmness while you wait for everything to get back to normal. You need multiple sources to avoid constantly drawing from the same one.

### If you see a pair of herons

The harmony in your romantic relationship is a source of mutual calm.

# Hippopotamus

Element: **water**
Season: **spring**
Keywords: **living space, inner light, protection**

In a way hippopotami are the bears of the savanna, unequivocally asserting their territory wherever they are. There are no two ways about it: no one goes through without their consent. The hippopotamus knows that in some situations the use of force is necessary to protect your integrity. This power animal teaches you that instead of dillydallying about getting others to respect your personal space, it is preferable to take the lead and vigorously defend that space.

## MESSAGE

Sometimes there is no point in trying to talk things through. If you are surrounded by toxic people and want to take back control of your life, you will at some point need to bare your teeth. There is no room for hesitation or doubt. The hippopotamus urges you to show no pity towards those who steal your energy. It will give you the strength to resist pressure and dare to protect your personal space and inner light.

# Hoopoe

Element: **air**

Season: **spring**

Keywords: **originality, appearance, rebel personality**

Hoopoes are quite unique, distinguished-looking birds, and with their feathered crowns and colourful appearance they brighten the landscape with their singularity. The hoopoe will appear to you if you are an atypical person who takes ownership of your rebel personality. You'll never be happy if you try to be like everyone else!

## MESSAGES

You don't like to have other people's tastes imposed on you. Fashion and its influence roll off you like drops of water off a duck, and the hoopoe encourages you in this affirmation of who you are. Your look showcases your personality. You know yourself well, and you understand that you can make good use of your singularity. If you still feel shy about your choices, the hoopoe invites you to start by wearing colourful clothes or unconventional accessories.

### Relationships

*If you are in a relationship*: you have chosen your partner well, as you are both very colourful people with unconventional, quirky personalities. Not everyone will like you, of course, but if you're comfortable with who you are then that's what counts!

*If you are single*: to attract an ideal partner you will need to show your deep colours. Try to remain true to yourself and don't seek to be like other people, as this is how people will notice you. Be bold, and wear creative clothes.

## Work

Many workplaces impose certain standards, such as a dress code. The problem is that it is difficult for you to thrive if you're not allowed to display a touch of your originality. Mindsets are evolving, though, and you can contribute to a change in attitude. Accessories will be your best asset to show your difference.

## Family

Your rebel personality has sometimes attracted misunderstandings or even the wrath of your family. You may have been strongly impacted by a feeling of being the ugly duckling in y our clan, yet you have shown yourself equal to forging your own personality within this context. This is why you now own who you are outside the family circle, which is all to your credit!

## Health

You are all fire and flame, a rebel momentum that can sometimes make you impulsive. Tolerance is your best ally to protect your liver from havoc wreaked by anger. Don't forget that your difference isn't a battle but a personal choice, so try not to get into conflicts with other people.

## SPECIAL MESSAGES

### If you see a hoopoe sitting still
Don't waste time trying to understand how others function. Take action in your own way, because up till now it seems to have served you well!

### If you see a hoopoe in flight
Release the feeling of being an ugly duckling and fly off into your own world.

### If you see a hoopoe in your garden
Your singular character is an asset to helping the world change. Stay true to yourself so you can show others the way.

# Horse

Element: **earth**

Season: **summer**

Keywords: **body and spirit in harmony, releasing beliefs, empowerment**

Horses are allies of your body and spirit. They are the mounts of your dreams, bringing your physical and spiritual bodies into harmony. In the face of danger horses react by fleeing, except when they decide to put their trust in humans to guide their way. The horse will appear to you when there are choices you need to make. Acting as a free human requires you to release the shackles of your limiting beliefs. What are you really capable of doing, and who can say aside from you?

## MESSAGES

Deep self-knowledge isn't given to everyone. You notice your minor thoughts and fastidiousness but neglect to observe the true potential you possess. Fear of failure, the ways others perceive you or mistaken beliefs make you unaware of who you truly are. The horse invites you to genuinely rediscover yourself to release the potential asleep inside you.

### Relationships

*If you are in a relationship*: take matters into your own hands. The one with whom you share your life is no longer the same person they were when you met, and neither are you. Get back in alignment with yourself and take stock of your personal and common evolution.

*If you are single*: the choice of living alone or not is yours. The horse invites you to recapture your freedom of action by eliminating mistaken beliefs about your ability to meet someone. Anything is possible; the reins are in your hands. Don't wait for this freedom to come from outside, as it is up to you to become aware of your choices.

## Work

Horses are social animals that are reassured by the presence of their herd, yet they are capable when guided by humans to go off and explore new territory. You might try breaking free from your hierarchy to venture into fresh fields. A short course or training program could enable you to find the courage to try a new activity.

## Family

Family fears and heritage forge your limiting beliefs and condition the choices you think you freely make. Be bold, and reflect on these shadows to give yourself more freedom of action. You minimise your potential: you are capable of so much more than you think!

## Health

Harmony throughout the physical body is connected with your thoughts and feelings. Body, spirit and soul are the three vehicles of what you resonate in this world. The horse is a mirror to help you align in your hearts with what you truly are, beyond judgement. If you start by putting an end to your self-judgements you'll gain in self-confidence and energy.

## SPECIAL MESSAGES

### If you see a horse

You are beginning to glimpse traits in your personality that you were unaware of, and the horse supports you in learning to become confident in what you can accomplish. Your spirit has no limits but the ones you set yourself.

### If you dream of a horse
A free spirit is someone who allows themselves to dream, even if it seems crazy. Let yourself be guided by your deep aspirations.

### If you fall off a horse
There are shadows to be released in order for your body and spirit to resonate in harmony with your heart. The horse supports you in taking full responsibility for your choices.

# Hummingbird

Element: **spirit**
Season: **summer**
Keywords: **creative thought, dreams, magic**

Hummingbirds are among the smallest birds on earth, and are able to hover in flight to gather nectar from flowers. Their energy is like a fairy's – glittery and magical – and they are connected with the element of spirit, for their action flows from the subtle realms into your reality. The hummingbird is a potentiator of dreams: each creative thought, no matter how small, grows at its touch. This power animal comes to you to remind you that the greatest discoveries are born from dreams. To help the earth evolve it is important to keep imagining the best.

## MESSAGES

The hummingbird knows that behind each invention is someone in pursuit of a dream. The world of tomorrow does not yet exist and it is up to you to create it, first through your thoughts and then through your actions. The hummingbird supports you in the materialisation of your hopes, and your optimism and idealism are what will make that possible. Work for the transformation of your world. The tiniest idea can come to life under the influence of the hummingbird.

### Relationships
*If you are in a relationship*: your imagination is full of hopes and dreams and nurtures your common projects. The hummingbird

perceives what shines in your heart and the purity of your intentions and acts like the tap of a magic wand to strengthen your desires. A wave of luck is in store for you.

*If you are single*: whatever your goal, you will receive a boost from the hummingbird. The wheel is turning in your favour and hope will accompany you on the path to personal fulfilment.

## Work

Everyone bears responsibility for the world of tomorrow, so your actions and choices have consequences. You are one of those optimistic people who wants to believe in human nature, so the hummingbird has crossed your path to give life to your beliefs in your reality. You are invited to be practical and consider your ideas as projects.

## Family

Future generations come bearing hopes and dreams. They are gifted with wisdom, respect for the world, awareness of all life and a desire to take care of the planet. Listen to the souls that have been entrusted to you, and help them walk their path towards the future while preserving the purity in their hearts. You are their guide in this life.

## Health

Your body is your vehicle to experiment with life. The more you nurture positive thoughts the more your body will follow. Good health is first cultivated in your mind, for your metabolism is influenced by the way you vibe. Shine out your light, as the hummingbird is showering magic powder on you.

## SPECIAL MESSAGES

### If you see a hummingbird

This is a sign of good luck. Things are going to get better and better for you and you are going to benefit from positive energy and take great leaps forward.

### If you dream of a hummingbird

You are nurturing a dream that deserves to come to life. You are an actor for the world of tomorrow, and the hummingbird has come to support you.

# Jaguar

Element: **fire**

Season: **autumn**

Keywords: **inner warrior, solitude, patience**

Renowned for their strength and power, jaguars represent the spirit of the warrior, the hunter full of courage and daring. When the jaguar appears to you it is to let a wild side of your being rise to the surface with a rush of life. Through the sun aspect of its masculine side the jaguar invites you to integrate your sacred dimension and go beyond the duality of masculinity in conflict with life.

## MESSAGES

Aligning with your deep, untamed side doesn't mean going completely wild, but finding the perfect balance between observation and action. This is the wisdom and patience that the jaguar wants to teach you. Your inner warrior needs to find its determination and pursue its goal without you scattering your focus. Take the time to focus your energy in accordance with the sun: when it sets, take the rest you need before diving into action again.

### Relationships

*If you are in a relationship*: jaguars are not very good at sharing, and for them having a partner isn't a priority. If you don't prioritise your relationship enough it may mean you need more time in your personal space before you can focus on your partner. Express your needs to be better understood by your partner and be respectful of your nature, as good balance in your relationship is at stake.

*If you are single*: you have the strength to live alone. For you, a partner isn't an end in and of itself but an opportunity to walk a path together while still maintaining your independence. If you meet someone, explain your position to them so they don't see it as running away, but rather as a true need. Your slightly impulsive nature isn't always completely understood.

## Work

You need to channel your energy rather than scattering it over too many projects, as it is by focusing your attention in a single direction that you will attain your goal. The jaguar is here to help you stay on course with strength and patience.

## Family

You are unpredictable, and your family doesn't always know how to approach you. Rather than diving into conflicts, try to clearly express the way you operate and your need for solitude. If necessary you can always decline some invitations to preserve your inner strength.

## Health

You have such strength and energy! To preserve this capital you need to abide by your biological clock and sleep cycle. Get enough sleep, and you will be able to move mountains.

## SPECIAL MESSAGES

### If you dream of a jaguar

You have a goal to achieve. Your state of mind as you face the jaguar in your dream is an indication of the position you need to take with respect to that goal. The jaguar will help you use your power to reach your potential.

## A SOOTHING KARMIC ENCOUNTER

During an animal communication session Charly the cat showed his human companion that he had been a jaguar in another life and she a hunter. Their meeting in this life had been absolutely magical, as though she was reconnecting with a part of herself but with a fear of her own power, embodied by the jaguar. She had killed him in that other life and condemned herself to never again shine with full power. Charly is now her guide to assist her in reconnecting with the sacred masculine inside her, the one that speaks from the heart.

# J

# Jay

Element: **earth**
Season: **spring**
Keywords: **protection, jealousy, truth**

Eurasian jays are very present in European forests, and the blue feathers they display on their sides make them very recognisable. Jays give a strident cry to warn other animals of an intruder's presence, and they are capable of imitating with great talent the shriek of a buzzard or the hoot of a tawny owl. These birds are jokers at heart, and they use their talent for imitation to take great fun in tricking other animals. Jays have a privileged relationship with oak trees, which provide jays with acorns to eat. In exchange, the birds disperse the seeds for miles around. Jays alone scatter around 4,600 acorns a year, so they are thus sentinels and protectors of the forest.

## MESSAGES

The jay's message is: 'Be like the oak tree, strong and stable. Offer your fruits, entrust them to me, and I will do the rest. I will take care to scatter them so they may come to life. I will take them to fertile lands, away from predators. I know how to trick ill-intentioned spirits. Offer yourself to life; you are protected.' This power animal invites you to accept its protection, as it wants to show you that in its presence your ideas or the projects of your heart will find a place of fulfilment if you consent to offer them to the world.

## Relationships

The jay has a message for everyone: 'Those whose hearts are pure will find treasures.'

*If you are in a relationship*: the jay invites you to be more authentic in your relationship. Don't hide any truth, or you may find yourself playing a particular role and losing your identity.

*If you are single*: don't be afraid to show your feelings and take off your mask, as it is only by being yourself that you will be able to find true love.

## Work

You may have ill-intentioned or jealous people around you or people who are playing a double game. Ask the jay to help you by making these people show their true colours. You are under the jay's protection and masks will soon come off, so pay attention.

## Family

Your role as a sentinel is to protect your family, so be observant and vigilant. The jay is taking it upon itself to send egotistical minds on the wrong track.

## Health

You have an important role to play within your family or work environment, and people count on you. Be true to yourself: even if you know how to easily adapt to your interlocutor, don't play a role. Don't be like a chameleon or you will lose part of your identity, and stay away from people who don't appear to be open and honest.

## SPECIAL MESSAGES

### If you find a blue jay feather

You have received the jay's protection, and it will support you in the days to come. Put the feather in your wallet or under your pillow so you can benefit from the jay's energy.

### If a jay takes flight before you
It is time to move away from people who do not respect you as you are. It can also be a sign that you need to put an end to a situation in which you have been feeling uncomfortable for a while.

### If a jay is sitting still before you
The jay is advising you to pay attention to your life, and in particular to your current questionings. Answers can only come if you take the time to observe your situation.

### If a jay cries in the sky above
The jay is warning you of potential danger from ill-intentioned or jealous people. Rest assured that you will receive insightful information when the time is right. You are protected in other, invisible realms.

### If you find a dead jay
You have reached the end of a toxic relationship with a friend, romantic interest, person at work or family member because your paths are diverging. You are urged to now distance yourself from this person. A new awareness will enable you to recover your zest for life and your personal space.

## A TERRIFYING MASK

I was about to leave for an evening of guided meditation that I facilitate when I saw a jay sitting on a branch. I heard the jay warn me about masks. During the meditation session, as I was entering into a trance with my shamanic drum and receiving messages from the souls that were present, one of the participants began to reveal a dark side to him, a terrifying mask. I felt the jay's protection, however, and it helped me accept this deep dimension and support the participant towards greater light.

# Jellyfish

Element: **water**
Season: **autumn**
Keywords: **inner compass, temporality, beat of the earth**

Jellyfish existed long before humankind made its first appearance. They seem to have got through the ages and be able to live outside of time. They have a very different constitution from mammals and possess a captivating, almost hypnotic way of moving with a reassuring, enveloping energy. The jellyfish will appear if you are in need of reconnecting with your primordial rhythm and inner compass.

## MESSAGES

The jellyfish asks you to set aside just for a moment the issues and hectic pace of your daily life to listen to your body's inner beat. What happens when you stop and the flow of your thoughts quietens down? Feel how perfect that instant is, and how it contains everything you need.

### Relationships

*If you are in a relationship*: the jellyfish invites you and your partner to take an inner journey together. Close your eyes and imagine that you are outside of time, in outer space or in the ocean. Take this journey together to rediscover your essentials: what matters most to both of you, about each other and in your relationship outside of daily life.

*If you are single*: time frightens you, as you feel that you are in a race against it when in reality it is only an illusion. Reflect on how you can slow time down and stretch it to make more room for your present moments. In this way you will be in a welcoming energy rather than waiting for a partner to show up.

## Work

You feel pressured to turn in completed projects or get tasks done on time. In the tumultuous context of your work environment, take five minutes to sit and observe everyone rushing about. Imagine that you are like a jellyfish: outside of time. Recharge your energy before returning with a greater sense of peace to your tasks for the day. These breaks aren't a waste of time; on the contrary, a rested brain works twice as well.

## Family

As time goes by family members are born and others pass away in the circle of life. In order not to feel that this is just to be endured, spend time with your loved ones. Plan a break from your schedule to visit people living further away and nurture relationships that will last well beyond your present incarnation.

## Health

Stress provokes an excessive production of cortisol, which has a direct impact on your body functions. The jellyfish invites you to find more time to rest, to connect with the jellyfish's wavelength and float in peace.

## SPECIAL MESSAGES

### If you dream of a jellyfish

Take time to rest, as you are tired out by your daily life. Don't be afraid to live at your own pace and change established rules.

### If you find a jellyfish on the beach

Your inner compass is looking to set a course. It is in the silence of your thoughts that you will be able to hear your own heartbeat.

J

### If you see a jellyfish in the water

You have the ability to live in many dimensions at once. Don't neglect the power of your dreams and thoughts.

### If you are stung by a jellyfish

It is time to move out of a state of lethargy in which you don't listen to your body and needs. You are guided by your mind, and it is disconnecting you from your deep yearnings. The jellyfish has come to forcefully restore this connection for you by giving you an electric shock!

## RECONNECTING WITH YOUR INNER RHYTHM

A young girl had come to me for a guided shamanic drumming session. She was looking for answers to questions about her future and the choices she needed to make so she journeyed into the depths of the ocean, where she met a jellyfish. It was a soothing and reassuring encounter. The jellyfish came to connect her with her inner compass and tell her that her choices were all inside her. The young girl's body was refusing to put on weight, which was something the jellyfish could help her with as it has a simple digestive cavity that acts as both stomach and intestines.

A dreamer who lived in her own world, this young girl reconnected with who she was and found her inner rhythm. A year later life circumstances brought her to live on the edge of the ocean, where she found a job and a new boyfriend. She continues to explore her path, and the jellyfish's wavelength still supports her in staying on course with the help of her inner compass.

# Kangaroo
## (and wallaby)

Element: **earth**

Season: **summer**

Keywords: **security, self-realisation, intrauterine life**

Kangaroos are marsupials. The females possess a belly pouch, a safe space in which their babies finish growing and preparing for the outer world. The kangaroo represents the protection you need to realise your potential. To make great leaps forward you need to have received enough attention to become self-confident. The kangaroo brings you back to your intrauterine experience and the baseline of security you needed but may not have received before embarking on the path of life.

## MESSAGES

A regression under hypnosis into your intrauterine life could help you recover a feeling of inner security and confidence so you can move towards a bright future. If this sort of therapy isn't your thing you can write to your inner child to reassure it. Your intrauterine environment was probably stressful. Identify the fears in the amniotic fluid surrounding you, and in your mother so you can move towards releasing them.

### Relationships

*If you are in a relationship*: you often need to be reassured by your partner, as though you constantly doubt their feelings for you, and this can become suffocating for them. You need to heal your insecurity for yourself because, in so doing, you will gain in personal independence.

*If you are single*: you have doubts about your potential to charm, and this insecurity can be felt by the people you meet. Put the odds in your favour by identifying your fears, which will enable the universe to bring you a healthy and positive encounter.

### Work

You often take two steps backward for each step forward. The kangaroo is bringing you positive energy, so move towards success and take ownership of your potential.

### Family

A secure, reassuring environment is essential for any child to develop their cognitive functions and trust in life. Unstable conditions push children to find protection through coping mechanisms. Reconnect with your inner child and give it the security it needs so you can move forward with greater serenity in your adult life.

### Health

Your anxiety and lack of self-confidence stem from emotional insecurity, and this inner instability has an impact on your body's energy. Skin issues or problems with sleep or related to your thyroid can appear when you are about to make a great leap forward.

## SPECIAL MESSAGES

### If you dream of a kangaroo

It is time to reconnect with the foetus you were before being born into this world. That foetus will help you understand your desire to incarnate on this earth and the choice you made with regard to this incarnation.

### If you see a kangaroo

You are ready to make a leap forward. Have faith, and run with great strides towards the next stage of your life!

# Kingfisher

Element: **water**
Season: **summer**
Keywords: **observation, action, uninhibitedness**

Kingfishers have a keen sense of observation. Perched on a branch, they wait for the opportune moment to seize their prey. They are able to dive underwater and can plunge well over one metre down, and despite their bright plumage their personality is quite discreet. The kingfisher will appear to you if you spend rather too much time thinking before taking action. It is wise to wait for the opportune moment, but not to the extent of letting an opportunity slip by you. You also need to know how to dive in and rid yourself of your fear so you can defend your projects.

## MESSAGES

You have the ability to observe and even to anticipate. Your avant-garde points of view are not always well showcased, because very often you don't dare give life to your ideas. It is only once someone else has gone on ahead of you that you realise you should have taken the plunge. The next opportunity will be the right one, as long as you don't overthink it and risk seeing the materialisation of your idea pass you by!

### Relationships

*If you are in a relationship*: you need time to be sure you're making the right choice before moving on to the next stage. Take care, however, as your partner could interpret this as fear of commitment. If you think for too long you will lose all spontaneity.

*If you are single*: you are waiting for an opportunity to present itself. The kingfisher has unlimited patience. What about you: do you want to wait? The kingfisher has come to ask you that question. If you need to let things come to you then waiting is the right attitude, but if you are tired of just hoping for something to happen then you are going to have to hop onto a different branch and change tactics.

## Work

You have the ability to anticipate currents and spot bargains and needs, but you don't tap into that ability because your doubts tend to catch up with you. Move forward with confidence and take action faster to get ahead of the competition.

## Family

You have inherited an introverted temperament that works against you when it comes to quickly taking the lead. Find a way to break free from that inherited timidity so you can extend your visionary talents.

## Health

When you don't seize an opportunity your entire self-confidence takes a hit. Don't feel guilty: bounce back quickly instead, for life has other surprises in store for you. Don't let those hesitant experiences make a dent in your enthusiasm.

## SPECIAL MESSAGES

### If you see a kingfisher perched on a branch
Waiting time is over, so take the plunge! There is an opportunity to be seized.

### If you dream of a kingfisher

It is time to change your way of doing things and believe in your potential. Your visionary talents need to be expressed.

### If you see a kingfisher dive into the water

You are ready to release your fears and follow the path that is opening before you. Be bold!

# Koala

Element: **earth**
Season: **summer**
Keywords: **understanding, peace, dialogue**

Koalas carry the energy of peace and work for non-violent communication. The koala is an ally for mediators and people who have an innate sense of dialogue. When the koala appears it is to remind you that you possess these talents and it is time to use them to change this world.

## MESSAGE

Words are power, and sharing a message of peace or love is a gift to the world. You have the capacity to bring others into dialogue and better understand each other, and you should use it for the greater good. You could also help humans and animals live together in greater harmony.

# L

# Ladybird

Element: **air**

Season: **summer**

Keywords: **inner child, wounds, metamorphosis**

Ladybirds are allies in the garden, keeping populations of undesirable insects under control and working with humans to maintain balance within the plant realm. Ladybirds are one of those animals that metamorphose into adulthood. They bring joy and hope: children marvel at them and many adults are fascinated by them. Still, don't be deceived by a ladybird's innocent appearance, as the spots on its outer wings aren't a sign of age. Rather, they are toxic, there to warn away predators. The ladybird reminds you that where there is light there are also shadows.

## MESSAGES

Your inner child is looking to make contact with you: when did you last listen to it? It's as though you had set aside a part of who you are, in all likelihood to protect yourself from the shadows of the past, but in burying that part you may also have lost your zest for life. The ladybird wants to help bring spontaneity and lightness into your heart. When this power animal appears it is to urge you into wonderment!

### Relationships

*If you are in a relationship*: the ladybird invites you to develop greater lightness and spontaneity in your relationship. Have fun and be imaginative, because it is by leaving the beaten path that you will find a second wind.

*If you are single*: the ladybird is bringing you a breath of hope. You will meet someone with whom you can enjoy life.

## Work

Your past failures or difficult experiences happened to help you find your place. It would be a good idea to think about collaborating with other professionals or entering into new alliances.

## Family

Your family is about to expand, perhaps through a birth, and this person coming into your life will bring a breath of fresh air and vitality.

## Health

The ladybird is asking you not to overlook your past painful experiences but to display them proudly. Your wounds and transformations have contributed to making you the person you are today. Bring joy into your life, and you will find new vitality.

## IT ALL DEPENDS ON THE COLOUR

Asian ladybirds are yellow while endemic species are red. Ladybirds possess a dual energy, which is why they have positive and negative sides even if they must be considered wholly. The negative aspect of yellow ladybirds is generally related to the aggressive and predatory side of your shadow, while red ladybirds evoke the emotional dimension of your shadow part. Depending on their colour, ladybirds come to you to address different types of wounds: the yellow ones invite you to focus on anger, and the red on scarcity. More positively, yellow ladybirds come bearing simple joy, while red ladybirds bring beauty and love of life.

# L

## SPECIAL MESSAGES

### If you take a ladybird in your hand to let it fly away

It is time to open your heart and wings to the magic of life, and to synchronicity. Reconnect with a child's wonder at nature's beauty. Make a wish, as you will be heard.

### If a ladybird lands on you

A person you love or who marked you in your childhood is paying you a visit, so embrace their message of love. It can also be a sign that someone is thinking about you.

### If a ladybird won't fly away

The ladybird is trying to bring something to your attention. Think about any questions you currently have to open your awareness to the ladybird's message. Something needs to emerge out of your child's heart.

---

## WHEN THOUGHTS MATERIALISE IN YOUR LIFE

I had been thinking about my sister-in-law, who loves ladybirds, when one appeared on my office window. Upon arriving home, another ladybird landed on my handbag, then as I was taking a walk a third decided to remain on me throughout. When I got home my phone began to ring. It was my sister-in-law, and of course I found the last ladybird sitting on the phone! Sometimes random thoughts just completely materialise in your life.

---

# Lamb

Element: **spirit**

Season: **spring**

Keywords: **purity, innocence, love, naïveté**

Lambs represent the purity and innocence embodied by newborns, and their white coats are associated with spirit and light. Their predators see them as easy targets, yet lambs possess immense inner strength: the strength of love. Their energy is that of a wide open heart . . . perhaps too much so. Lambs have to learn not to trust just anyone, and their life lesson is a hard one because they are so sensitive they can sometimes feel unable to ensure their own protection. If you encounter the energy of the lamb you must learn to accept duality.

## MESSAGES

When the lamb appears to you it is to speak about your choice of incarnation and your difficulty in grounding yourself in a dual world. Your sensitivity and empathy prevent you from harming others and your soul is deeply pure; however, we live in a world full of predators and you may sometimes feel defenceless. The lamb wants to help you deploy your own defences while still keeping an open heart. Accepting your own duality will be your first protection, because light and shadow must coexist for there to be balance. By remaining lucid you will be able to exercise vigilance and avoid trusting others blindly.

# L

### Relationships

*If you are in a relationship*: the lamb is here to witness the purity of your love. It wants you to protect this relationship from people who try to cause you harm. Don't listen to bad advice and gossip; listen to your heart!

*If you are single*: you feel that finding 'the one' is like searching for a needle in a haystack, yet beautiful souls find and attract each other as long as they keep an open heart and pay attention to the signs that come their way. Rather than throwing your hat in the ring of the first person you meet, keep faith in life.

### Work

The workplace sometimes appears like a jungle in which you can sense many dangers. Trust in your ability to defend yourself in the event of a problem, and conscientiously avoid all power-hungry people.

### Family

Your family is your refuge, but it can also be your personal hell. Finding your place and having the boldness to say what doesn't work for you can be difficult. Express yourself freely, for you are in your safe zone. Feel that you are loved and that there is no danger in expressing negative emotions.

### Health

The stress in your environment is proving harmful to your health. You are like an emotional sponge, and sometimes you just overflow. It would be a good idea for you to isolate yourself from time to time so you can take stock and sift through the information of the day.

## SPECIAL MESSAGES

### If you dream of a lamb

You have your full and rightful place on earth. Become aware of your own qualities and be willing to live fully, because you deserve it so much.

## If you see a lamb

There is a choice before you that is offering you an opportunity to assert yourself. If you decide to follow what you deeply want you will make no mistake. Trust in yourself.

# Lion

Element: **fire**

Season: **summer**

Keywords: **leadership, strength, aura**

As the king of the animal kingdom the lion represents strength and leadership. Lions shine with solar energy and their auras beam out around them, naturally commanding respect. The lion will appear to you if you are afraid to shine your light to help you take your rightful place in the world. Like the lion you are gifted with charisma, and you can be a source of inspiration to others.

## MESSAGES

You have made progress on your path and know your strength. The lion wants to urge you to reveal this inner work you have done and the light you have found inside you. It is time to bring all you have built into alignment, all the skills and the knowledge of the bright being you are that can shine in the world. Don't be afraid to extend this strength as it cannot cause harm; it is healthy because you have taken the time to discover it. By being ready to shine you will encourage others to do the same.

### Relationships

*If you are in a relationship*: a lion knows how handsome he is and is prone to taking advantage of it. Don't overdo your seduction tactics with your partner or you might wear them out. You can sometimes be a bit lazy and you like to be coddled, so take care not to become macho in your use of strength!

*If you are single*: you like to charm and may have trouble committing to a long-term relationship. You need constant reassurance about your looks, and the lion invites you not to indulge in such superficial relationships but to try to go further in an encounter that will have the capacity to move you differently.

## Work

Taking power may be something that frightens you. You are under the impression that you will need to fight to carve out a new place for yourself, and part of that fight is happening inside you. If you are bold and reveal your strength, what you say will be much more convincing. Your place will soon change in your work structure, and the more you accept this change the quicker you will find a new, more fulfilling role.

## Family

A lion depends for his own survival on his lionesses' ability to hunt. If you are living with someone, don't shirk domestic duties and don't forget that you are stronger together. Remember to thank the invisible help you get on a daily basis.

### Health

A lion's health depends on his capacity to shine. If a situation is preventing you from expressing your potential, if you cannot be seen, you run the risk of enduring chronic exhaustion and recurring headaches related to the solar energy that has no way of spreading throughout your aura. That energy will build up in your physical body and drain your reserves.

## DIFFERENCES BETWEEN THE LION AND THE LIONESS

The lioness has a much more sociable personality than the lion. She is the skilled head of the family, organising and planning everyone's duties. Without her there can be no stability in the group. The lioness represents the light of the home, but it is important not to reduce her to this role or that light will fade. The lioness has a deep sense of leadership and entrepreneurship.

## SPECIAL MESSAGES

### If you dream of a lion

Don't be afraid to inspire by taking on more responsibilities. You have the shoulders and charisma for it.

### If you dream of a lioness

Your family is important and you protect your loved ones with fervour, but don't forget to set that role aside once in a while to put your skills in the service of your other passions.

# Lizard

Element: **spirit**
Season: **spring**
Keywords: **inner weather, emotions, sunlight**

Lizards are cold-blooded animals that need a lot of sun to warm up their organs, and they know that their well-being depends on the elements and outside temperatures. The lizard invites you to also become aware of the influence of sunlight on your mood. Humankind needs sunlight; it provides vitamin D to your body and influences your inner weather. The sun always comes back out after the rain, so you need to accept changes in the weather outside as much as in your emotions. They have a purpose and make sunny days even more beautiful.

## MESSAGES

It is because life arouses many emotions in you that you know how to appreciate joy and moments of grace, and it is because you have known pain that you can recognise joy when it floods your heart. Accept every emotion that flows through you: they teach you how to appreciate life. If the weather was always wonderful would you realise how lucky you are?

### Relationships

*If you are in a relationship*: a life together is never without bumps along the way. If you think that you will only experience the best, you have another think coming. Like a small boat, a relationship is always subjected to waves and it is through facing storms together that you will understand the strength of your union.

*If you are single*: the problem with casual flings is that you only ever see the best aspects of another person without ever having to accept any bad sides, but when you dream of the ideal partner you forget that it is a part of life to experience ups and downs. Whatever the case, the lizard invites you to reflect on the reality of a relationship and its range of emotions.

## Work

It is possible to like your job yet sometimes reflect on it and call some aspects into question. Beware of dream peddlers who claim to live each day in harmony. The atmosphere at work is like the weather: more or less mild depending on the day. Try not to idealise things but rather to accept that this variability exists in all lines of work.

## Family

In every family there are tensions, secrets and, on occasion, tragedies. Let emotions find ways of expression as they come, as it will be good for your children. Teach your children that every emotion has a purpose, that there is nothing to be ashamed of.

## Health

When you conceal an emotion it will inevitably backfire on you. Anger attacks your liver and stomach, fear freezes the energy in your kidneys, resentment impairs your heart functions and sadness damages your lungs. Each organ is connected with an emotion, so learn to express each emotion without judgement. There are no positive or negative emotions: the only negative thing would be to hold them back.

## SPECIAL MESSAGES

### If you see a green lizard

Great, wonderful emotions are on the way. Let yourself be carried by your inner weather so that it may guide you towards a rainbow!

### If a lizard comes into your house

It is within your home that you have trouble expressing your emotions. Plan for times of sharing during which everyone will have an opportunity to say what they feel. If this is too difficult for some people, it can sometimes be easier to write things down.

### If your cat brings back a dead lizard

You need to stop idealising everything, such as the perfect person, perfect family or perfect job. These things only exist on social media, and in real life we all feel the same things. Emotions are universal: we all cry in the same way in every country in the world, just as we all celebrate the important moments. If you experience these things more strongly than others it is a gift! You are like an artist to whom a greater palette of colours has been given, so learn to discover the richness of all the emotions in your palette.

## LIVING WITH LIZARDS

This is Dorothée's story: 'A family of lizards had been living around our patio for two years. The first summer they fled as soon as we opened the window. The following year, as I was finishing my training in canine and equine shiatsu and opening myself up to animal communication, I found the lizards to be less fearful. I decided to try to communicate with one of them, listen to it and ask it if it was happy living with us. I learned that this particular lizard was called Kvar.

'This encounter happened at a time when I had many questions about my child's hypersensitivity as well as my future in shiatsu for animals. In the end the lizard family's presence helped me better understand my child's sensitivity and begin to see the new doorways that were opening within me and enabling me to listen to the energy of the ones we call cold-blooded animals, so that I could use this energy to access a more subtle level of information during my healing sessions.'

# Llama

Element: **earth**

Season: **spring**

Keywords: **sense of humour, self-deprecation, tolerance**

The llama has a sense of humour, loves jokes and wants to take you into their world, in which they enjoy life and savour every moment. Llamas do have one fault, which is that they are not very tolerant. Laughing at others is one thing, but laughing at yourself is another. The llama will appear to you if you need to develop a sense of self-deprecation in your everyday life.

## MESSAGES

A critical mind often leads you to judge. It is normal to compare yourself with others, and it sometimes helps you to see yourself in a clearer light. However, you are invited now to take life lightly and with a dash of humour. Make light of your situation by making fun of it: you will see that the spirit of the llama can help you laugh at anything!

### Relationships

*If you are in a relationship*: you can be a bit touchy when your partner makes a comment about something to do with you. Don't take things so personally, and the atmosphere will lighten up considerably. With a little humour you can send your reply gently on its way!

*If you are single*: not taking yourself seriously and knowing how to laugh at yourself is a real advantage when trying to meet someone. It makes you so much more human and endearing, and humour always breaks the ice quickly. Use that asset to charm.

### Work

There is room for humour and self-deprecation in the workplace. By opening that door you will help others develop a more casual attitude and will gain in popularity.

### Family

Family meals sometimes want for that touch of self-deprecation that makes an atmosphere more relaxed. Don't fire up immediately when you feel targeted; learn to take things with a lighter heart. In the mind of the llama, life is fun!

### Health

You need to laugh every day, especially in situations that aren't at all funny. The energy of laughter calms and oxygenates your mind, and gives it the positivity it absolutely needs to move forwards when things are complicated.

## SPECIAL MESSAGES

### If you see a llama
Laugh at yourself, at your appearance, and distance yourself from any judgements others may make about you. The important thing is to be able to see things in a more lighthearted way.

### If you dream about a llama
Humour is your best weapon to face life's ordeals.

# Lynx

Element: **fire**
Season: **winter**
Keywords: **introspection, retreat, humility**

Lynxes are shy animals. Their reticence allows them to live far from the tumult of the human world, in a dimension protected from chaos where the reality of life simply vibes. The lynx invites you to retreat and introspect, and to have the humility to live in a world where happiness is within reach.

## MESSAGES

If you have too many dreams you will move away from your primary goals, your key objectives. You will always want more, and sometimes you forget to see how rich your daily life is. The lynx invites you to engage in introspection and focus on the simple, unvarnished gifts life brings. Perhaps you could find true happiness in those things?

### Relationships

*If you are in a relationship*: projects are important, but constant projections into the future make you forget to live in the present. Simple moments are a source of joy so savour them, because they are so precious!

*If you are single*: perhaps the partner you are looking for doesn't exist in the way you imagine but is already right beside you, with a different appearance. Sometimes you go looking elsewhere for what is already right under your nose!

# L

### Work

Everyone knows that the grass is always greener on the other side of the fence. The lynx invites you to release that point of view and live in acceptance of your daily life. By letting go you will find new sources of joy.

### Family

Each day is an opportunity to share and be joyful. Everything is within your reach, and you only have to stretch out your hand to take it.

### Health

Why complicate things when they can really be quite simple? Don't search for exotic alternatives for your health and avoid changes in your diet. Reconnect with your common sense, as your body is telling you what it needs. The best remedies are often the simplest ones.

## SPECIAL MESSAGES

### If you dream of a lynx

Reconnect with simple things. Develop a new taste for real rather than virtual pleasures in your daily life, as the lynx is urging you to follow this path.

### If you see a lynx

You have a rare ability to see the bright side of things. It is a gift, so share it with the people around you.

# Magpie

Element: **air**
Season: **winter**
Keywords: **curiosity, superficial world**

Magpies love anything that shines, to the extent that they can let themselves wallow in illusions in a superficial world, and have a tendency to accumulate objects. They are very extroverted birds with a great need to express themselves, and are just as mischievous as they are intelligent. The magpie will appear to you if you need to remember that being is more important than having.

## MESSAGES

You like to be seen and make your voice heard, and this is an asset in your efforts to share your thoughts and communicate with others; however, the magpie invites you to take up a real challenge. Don't delude yourself as to what you want to have; instead, bring your entire being into resonance without falling into traps laid by your ego. Some people may find the magpie a bit mercenary, but its attraction to things that shine isn't a vice and just reflects its need for recognition.

### Relationships

*If you are in a relationship*: the intention in which a gift is given is greater proof of the giver's love for the recipient than the gift's actual monetary value. Something that has been made by hand with love can be as priceless as a diamond.

*If you are single*: it can be tempting to seek out a good match with someone who could provide you with material and financial security. However, you need to ask yourself if this is the most important thing. Being a social success on the arm of an important person might be flattering, but would it really fill your need to be loved?

## Work

Greed can sometimes make you take leave of your senses and forget the meaning of things. Money is energy, a means of exchange, that needs to flow, so learn to let go.

## Family

Scarcity may have generated a desire to possess things. Your need to show others that you are financially secure reveals a certain emotional fragility, and this weakness can alienate you from personal fulfilment. Don't forget that your mission is to release your fear of scarcity so your entire being may shine out into the world.

## Health

An accumulation of objects can disturb the energy in your house, and yours in the process. If you reconnect with the meaning of 'essentials' by giving away things you no longer have any use for there will be a better flow of energy in your house.

## SPECIAL MESSAGES

### If you see a magpie
Don't get lost in material dreams, as you probably don't want for essentials. Notice how rich and self-sustaining your world is.

### If you hear a magpie sing
Use your capacity for expression to share your values. Your words are like a channel leading from your soul.

# Mole

Element: **earth**
Season: **spring**
Keywords: **mystery, sensory world**

Moles have very limited eyesight, which is why they use their other senses to find their way underground. Their senses of smell, touch and hearing are particularly developed and their energy is subterranean in quality, as moles know the depths of the earth and its mysteries. The mole invites you to enter into a more sensory world and reconnect with the real taste of things.

## MESSAGES

You are invited to explore your environment as though you were unable to see it and just smell, taste and touch it. You can focus on the softness of a piece of velvet fabric, for instance, or the smell of a piece of fruit or the flavour of a dish. By making an effort to satisfy each of your senses you will bring greater pleasure into your life.

### Relationships

*If you are in a relationship*: you are invited to look at your partner from a different angle. Take the opportunity of an evening together to get to know each other all over again using all your senses except your eyesight. Let your imagination run wild.

*If you are single*: the mole is your ally when reconnecting with pleasure. Sharing a good meal, warm moment or kiss are all pleasurable things you can allow yourself to feel again.

### Work

Let your flair guide you. Listen to that little voice inside you that knows whether it is worth it or not to engage in a new project or path, and try to trust in what you feel. The important thing is for you to be able to be yourself.

### Family

Touching the people you love and taking them into your arms is a simple pleasure but also an essential one, for your time on earth is ephemeral. To understand this is to know life's fragility and true beauty. Make the most of spending time with your loved ones.

### Health

You can feel when something is out of order in your body. Listen to your feelings so you can be ready to take immediate action. A warning is exactly that, and the quicker a disorder is treated the quicker it will be resolved. Don't wait for your symptoms to worsen before you act.

## SPECIAL MESSAGES

**If you have molehills in your garden**
You need to support your body by changing your health lifestyle.

**If you see a mole**
Your five senses are your best source of pleasure. Enrich your experiences by focusing entirely on your feelings.

# Monkey

Element: **air**

Season: **spring**

Keywords: **collective, social relations, group energy**

Monkeys are the animals that bear the greatest physical resemblance to us and they reflect what we have lost in our Western way of life: the richness of social relations. There are so many species of primates that it is difficult to draw general conclusions, but their energy does convey the power of the group. A monkey will never live long if it is alone; it needs its peers to survive. As a human you also need to reconnect with the power of the collective.

## MESSAGES

Ego complicates the relationships you have with other people. You may have forgotten that once upon a time we all lived together in caves. You can call upon this group dynamic when the monkey appears to you, because it has come to show you that you are stronger with others. Whatever your goal or the problem you want to solve, you can ask for help.

### Relationships

*If you are in a relationship*: you want to manage your problems alone, but by trying to control all aspects of your relationship you leave no room for your partner to relieve you of your tensions. The monkey knows that sexual energy has powerful, natural anti-anxiety properties, and it uses that energy to resolve conflicts. You might as well combine business with pleasure!

*If you are single*: if you really want to meet someone, why don't you ask your friends to invite you along to situations where you could provoke destiny? Who knows: one of them might already know the perfect person for you. You are not alone in your quest, so let people who love you give you a hand.

## Work

You will always go further together than when you walk alone. See how you can combine everyone's skills to forge a common direction. You can do it.

## Family

You can draw incredible strength from your family environment. Different generations helping each other will always generate a lot of joy. You are invited to develop those family ties to pass that unity down to the young people of your clan.

## Health

Your fatigue and stress levels depend on your ability to ask your loved ones for help. Learn to delegate tasks in order not to carry all the weight by yourself. Remember that you will be even more efficient together.

## SPECIAL MESSAGES

### If you dream of a monkey
You need to reconnect with the strength of the group, so issue a call for proposals.

### If you see a monkey
Someone in your close circle is an ally for your projects.

# Mosquito

Element: **spirit**
Season: **summer**
Keywords: **emotions, energies, resources**

Mosquitoes possess an incredible capacity for survival and adaptation: they are invaders, and nothing can stop them. Their energy is very sensitive to variations in frequency, and some people pay for this because they have a great many emotions swirling inside them. Their weakest energy points attract mosquitoes.

## MESSAGE

If you are regularly attacked by mosquitoes you are probably one of those people whose energy changes a lot in the course of the day. You pay the cost of being an emotional sponge. The mosquito has come to show you how important it is to take time to recharge your energy, alone, for greater inner peace.

# Mouse

Element: **earth**

Season: **autumn**

Keywords: **fear, comfort zone, action**

Mice are discreet, timid creatures that live in hidey holes inaccessible to predators because they are aware of being potential prey. Their strength lies in numbers and their ability to reproduce quickly to ensure their species' survival. Mice never dillydally: if they took their time about things they would risk their lives.

## MESSAGES

Sometimes you need to stop acting like prey or a victim so you can take up your place in this world. You need to stop hiding, hugging walls and avoiding making noises, because if you don't dare confront the world and its dangers you will never leave your comfort zone. It is time to increase your pace and venture out of your current environment.

### Relationships

*If you are in a relationship*: the mouse wants to show you that the healthiest type of relationship is one in which both parties are responsible for their own well-being. Don't expect your partner to offer what you cannot give yourself, and let your partner responsibly heal what concerns them.

*If you are single*: you have been marked by your past experiences. To seize the new opportunities that life has in store for you, you need to release the victim stance you are stuck in. You can be who you like; it's only a question of your inner attitude. The mouse invites you to leave your hidey hole.

### Work

Taking on responsibilities is a source of stress for you, yet you are so gifted! However, you do have a tendency towards self-sabotage. You are the only thing keeping you from climbing your career ladder, so do something important for yourself and reconnect with your self-confidence.

### Family

Some wounds are deep and condition your relationships with other people. When those wounds prevent you from taking the lead in your life it is time to say goodbye to them. The mouse will help you become an adult and take full responsibility for your happiness.

### Health

Your way of seeing the world conditions your state of mind and your body's reactions. When you are afraid your body curls up and shrinks, but when you let it open up into fulfilment it shines brilliantly. Let it show you the way.

## SPECIAL MESSAGES

### If you see a mouse

What responsibility have you entrusted to others when it is yours to own? The saying about if you want something done right you have to do it yourself should inspire you.

### If you find mice in your house

A new horizon in taking shape, and a decision will help you take ownership of your choice. Whatever your questions, the mouse reminds you that you are responsible for your own choices.

## If you find mice in your garage or basement

Something concerning your inner child is blocking your path. A hypnosis session could help you reconnect with your childhood fears so you make your way forward serenely.

## If you find mice in your attic

The roots of what may be blocking your path go back to your ancestors. You are invited to shed light on unfulfilled dreams and disillusions in your family to make greater room for your desires.

## If your cat brings you a mouse

You let your choices be influenced by others. The mouse would like to gently remind you that you are responsible for your inner freedom.

## If you are the owner of pet mice

Your mice are helping you soothe your fear of growing by showing you that when you leave your cage you learn from your experiences. Don't forget that your life is yours.

## A SIGN OF LIBERATION

During a training session on the inner child a mouse slipped into the room and took position behind the head of a woman stretched out on the floor in meditation. The mouse stayed there, utterly fearless, even washing itself a little, then left before the woman opened her eyes. That woman desperately needed to leave the hiding place she had shut herself up in for so long, attracting all sorts of situations that affirmed her victim's stance. Her inner child needed reassurance for her to finally dare to start forward with confidence in her life.

# Nightingale

Element: **air**

Season: **summer**

Keywords: **romanticism, poetry, love**

Nightingales sing about love. These birds are gifted with poetic souls, and sprinkle notes of romance onto your path. The nightingale invites you to let yourself be soothed by words that fill your heart. It knows that love is a form of exchange, and that giving freely is just as enchanting as receiving.

## MESSAGE

Your soul is in search of poetry, beauty and romance. If the one you love isn't very talented when it comes to wooing you, use your gifts to strike a chord in them. It will be a pleasure for you, and you will probably start an exchange.

# Octopus

Element: **spirit**
Season: **winter**
Keywords: **adaptability, intelligence, curiosity**

Octopi are mysterious, secret beings that like to hide away from curious eyes. Their inquisitiveness, however, can be so strong it sometimes leads them to take risks so they can explore the world. Their energy reveals a keen intellect, as they take time to observe before leaping into action. With their ability to melt into new territory, octopi represent a level of adaptability and flexibility from which you can draw inspiration.

## MESSAGES

The octopus urges you to open your mind and let go of judgement. Your curiosity is what enables you to overcome your fears, and the octopus supports you in adapting to a new situation. You have the inner resources to turn this change in circumstances into an opportunity for growth.

### Relationships

*If you are in a relationship*: use your capacity to adapt when you and your partner have different points of view. Once you understand them, these differences will no longer be obstacles between you.

*If you are single*: it is important to get to know another person as they truly are before diving into a relationship. Take time to observe situations and overcome your fears, because then you will be able to explore new horizons.

O

## Work

Everyone has two sides, one that is displayed to all and another, more discreet but often more authentic side. By drawing inspiration from the octopus you will learn to better understand your colleagues and clients in their truth, and you won't need to rely on appearances. This effort will enable you to flexibly melt into your work environment and take more relevant action.

## Family

Some people in your close circle know who you truly are, but there are others who may have trouble fully understanding you. You are secretive because you wish to preserve your privacy, and others wonder about you. You are right to take time to develop authentic and durable relationships, because once someone has gained your trust they can count on you in any circumstance!

## Health

When your fears take over you may suffer from anxiety, even to the extent of being a little paranoid, but if you identify and master your fears you will be able to let your curiosity lead you to new encounters at your own pace. Trust in life!

## SPECIAL MESSAGES

**If you dream of an octopus**
You want to explore new territory but you are afraid. Don't let your doubts smother your curiosity; just take time to think things through and look at all aspects of a situation before taking action.

**If you see an octopus**
A discovery awaits you. Let it come to you, and dive in as soon as your heart gives you the green light. Your yearnings are what will lead you out of your hiding place.

# Ostrich

Element: **air**
Season: **winter**
Keywords: **change, help, taking flight**

Ostriches have an almost prehistoric appearance. They are unable to fly because of their weight, yet their power is connected with the element of air because they are able to capture the energy of this element and maintain it on earth. The ostrich is an ally for anyone who wishes to leave a situation but still feels incapable of flying.

## MESSAGE

Before contemplating a change it is better to ask the right questions and focus on what is most important. Through its ancestral energy the ostrich takes you into your deepest desires: it's as though this power animal wants to bring you a great breath of fresh air in a complicated situation to help you see things more clearly. Soon you will be able to fly!

# Otter

Element: **water**
Season: **spring**
Keywords: **play, fun, inner child**

Otters are joyful, playful, sociable creatures that love to spend time with their peers. Their energy is rather like that of an adult who has managed to keep their child's heart. Play is at the centre of the otter's focus. This power animal invites you not to lose your capacity to have fun in life, as becoming an adult does not mean that you have to only see the serious side of things and set aside your playfulness.

## MESSAGES

You love to laugh and play: it is in your nature, except your daily life brings you serious issues to deal with far too often. The otter reminds you to set aside time in your calendar for fun moments, an important way to avoid sinking into gloom.

### Relationships

*If you are in a relationship*: intimate moments are the perfect time to indulge in fun and sexy games with your partner. Laughter and lightheartedness will make joyful memories of these moments.

*If you are single*: going out, dancing and having fun are the best ways to meet someone and create a bond. You will immediately know if you are on the same wavelength or not.

### Work

A party with your colleagues or a fun outing could help you forge ties within your team as you spend time together outside of your work environment. You could also try a musical or sports challenge or an equicoaching session for variety.

### Family

Within your family is an ideal space for play, and board games and fun outings are shared moments that will give new strength to your bond. Intergenerational reunions are, of course, greatly recommended!

### Health

You would like to participate in fun, pleasant activities but you deprive yourself of that pleasure because of your physical condition. Do your best to stay in shape, as you are never too old to start exercising and especially for a good reason!

## SPECIAL MESSAGES

### If you see an otter

Where has that playful side of yours gone? If you are willing to move out of your dejected state and reconnect with your joyful inner child you will recover a happier spirit.

### If you dream of an otter

It is time to take a break from your routine by organising an unusual outing.

O

# Owl

Element: **spirit**
Season: **winter**
Keywords: **wisdom, faith, future**

Owls are full of wisdom: they know that the sun always comes back after the rain, and they have an unshakeable faith in life. The owl comes to pass on this strength if you are wondering about the meaning of your life. This power animal has access to the doors of time and it knows the future. Of course, it will refrain from sharing this knowledge so you can make discoveries for yourself.

## MESSAGES

You doubt your life path; it is even possible those words hold no meaning for you. The owl has come to help you keep faith in your personal path. Whatever ordeals you may have experienced and may still be going through, the owl knows that the sun is just beyond those clouds. If you have faith in that, you will be able to make enlightened choices that will give you access to that light.

### Relationships

*If you are in a relationship*: the story of your meeting was already written, and the owl knew that you had a love to share. Let the sacred character of your union fill it with even more light. Your love is beautiful!

*If you are single*: the future is taking you towards the sun. The owl knows that the quest for true love requires having faith in your destiny. Souls are destined to meet when they are ready.

### Work

Keep faith if you have project, because with a little patience you will be able to attain your goal. Don't get discouraged along the way, as the owl already knows there is a happy ending for you.

### Family

Whatever quarrels or disagreements you are undergoing, a calmer way is possible. The future holds greater harmony for you.

### Health

If you or one of you loved ones is in ill health, know that the owl brings hope. Pray if you like, have faith in whatever happens and share this energy around you, as it will be indispensable for healing.

## SPECIAL MESSAGES

### If you hear an owl

You have a good support system in your life. The owl is bringing you the message that you need to keep hoping.

### If you find an owl feather

Prayer is simply a request, a wish, and faith and hope are what enable you to wait for the answer. Ask and you will be heard!

### If you find a dead owl

It is time to leave the past and negative thinking behind you. Faith is what calls light to shine. Trust in the future and find nourishment in your hopes, as they will bring new momentum to your life.

### If you see an owl

You are going to learn more about your life path. If you don't know what you have come on earth to do, the owl will send useful insights your way.

# Owl, barn

Element: **spirit**
Season: **winter**
Keywords: **intuition, transformation, alignment**

The barn owl will appear to you if you are experiencing major change: not a small, one-time transformation but a profound mutation involving accepting every part of what you vibe. The barn owl listens to all your intuitions, all your wishes, and knows when you are aligned with what you want. This power animal comes to tell you that it is good to be bold and make a leap of faith, landing on solid ground with your feet firmly planted on the earth. The barn owl's energy can be silent and furtive, just like the thoughts that arise in your mind, or loud and insistent when it is time for you to become aware of this process of transformation.

## MESSAGES

The barn owl has appeared to show you how far you've come and the alignment you have succeeded in creating between your thoughts and actions. The barn owl invites you to take time for retrospection before engaging in new projects, because change will come and faster than you think. Have a short break and take stock to see how you have managed to vibe all that you are in your life. This alignment allows you to consider your projects serenely, because your thoughts vibe with your heart.

## Relationships

*If you are in a relationship*: your life together has evolved in the right way, and it is now based on exchange and sharing. Take time to see what has enabled it to grow this way. Readjustments are necessary to experience the true depth of love.

*If you are single*: something has changed in you, and you are better aligned with your willpower. Take some distance from your previous relationships before diving into the unknown. The barn owl supports you in this evolution.

## Work

Your work is a great construction site inside you. You can sometimes find yourself a bit lost in this mental brouhaha, yet on many occasions you have shown yourself able to change paths. Look how your thoughts have always set you on your path and are increasingly guiding you on a way of the heart. The barn owl comes to validate this attitude of listening and action.

## Family

You perceive lots of unsaid things and have the ability to lift the veil on the secrets in your family. Keep working to free speech on all these things, as it has opened the door to great evolution on a personal level and in your family and produced a positive effect around you, enabling you to live in better alignment with your values.

## Health

It is time to release your bad habits so you can feel more in harmony with your body. The barn owl can help you recast an addiction or a form of compulsive behaviour, as long as you become aware of the consequences of your thoughts. Adopting a positive attitude will help you succeed in this.

## AMAZING SYNCHRONICITY

This is Charlotte's story: 'I was driving through the forest when I saw a barn owl take flight and head directly into my windshield. My heart was hammering and I thought I had killed it, but when I stopped the car and got out to check there was no sign of the owl. The next day I found wing dust on my windshield and a few scratch marks, so it hadn't been a dream. A few days later it started snowing: white flakes falling everywhere and transforming the outer world along with my inner landscape. That's when I understood I was invited to shed light on what was still in shadow and reveal who I truly was. I was being told that I was healed and that now everything was clear, smooth and simple, like the snow surrounding me.

'There certainly was a before and after that December. My last month of unemployment was over, and I was finally endeavouring to create my own company. Incredible barn owl! I had actually come across two others the preceding week that had taken wing before me in the woods. What an amazing synchronicity!'

## SPECIAL MESSAGES

### If you see a barn owl

A change in point of view will bring you in alignment with your actions and thoughts. A situation is going to evolve in a positive way, so trust in your intuition.

### If you hear a barn owl

Take time to see the change that has happened inside you and appreciate your alignment with the energy in your heart.

### If you see a barn owl that has been run over by a car

The past is behind you and you can move forward in all confidence. Going back is impossible, because you are on the path to self-knowledge.

### If a barn owl has made its nest on your property

You are giving more room to your intuition and it is helping you be more and more in harmony with your inner voice. This sensitive part of you is going to become more important in your life.

## A WISE WARNING

S. was admitted to hospital after thinking he might have had a heart attack. Thankfully for him, it was only a warning. On the way home with his wife in the middle of the night, S. almost hit a barn owl. The owl had come to warn him that an imminent change in his thought patterns was going to help him release his bad habits, and prompted S. to start work on rebalancing his diet. Through his new awareness he was able to improve his health.

# Panda

Element: **fire**

Season: **spring**

Keywords: **digestive system, food, assimilation**

Pandas feed on bamboo leaves because they have trouble assimilating other types of food. They actually have the same digestive system as carnivores, with only one stomach, but they have had to adapt to survive. The panda's energy is associated with the element of fire, which helps establish compensation mechanisms when a situation or environment has become inadequate.

## MESSAGES

Eating is full of meaning: it is all about giving your body the nutrients it needs to function and regenerate. This seems to be the message of the panda, who has found ways in the course of its evolution to adapt its eating habits to its environment. Think about the relationship you have with food. How do you digest your meals? How do you store the calories you take in? Could eating be a means of filling a void? You need to stop adapting to an unhealthy environment and change your outlook! The way you assimilate food depends on your capacity to digest the events of the day.

### Relationships

*If you are in a relationship*: you or your partner may have weight issues or a digestive disorder. You may be trying to adopt better eating habits but to no avail. You can't do it alone: your partner needs to be involved and support you. It is very important to understand that successful changes also depend on your environment.

*If you are single*: a lack of love can make you look for compensation in food. The problem is that self-confidence doesn't rise in proportion to your weight. Eating habits are only the tip of the iceberg, so you need to find help to understand what coping mechanisms lead you to your deleterious eating behaviours.

## Work

You are overwhelmed by daily events, and instead of releasing them you have a tendency to store them up inside. You may sometimes explode with anger, and people don't understand why. If you never release your stress your digestive system or weight curve runs a real risk of reacting to that inner storm. 'Everything is connected,' says the panda!

## Family

Your family relationships may reflect the panda's environment in the sense that they may be too adaptive. Emotional deprivation or problems related to a toxic relationship have affected you in the past. Become aware that it is up to you to modify this atmosphere so that you may create a family in your image, and then you will no longer need to adapt.

## Health

Your repressed emotions are affecting your metabolism and digestive system. You are compensating for something, and you are strongly urged to understand where the malaise is coming from before trying to resolve its physical consequences. Take the causes in your environment into account, or any effort you make will be unsuccessful.

### If you dream of a panda

It is time to release what led your body to compensate for a lack. Be it emotional, material or related to your environment, that lack belongs to the past. You are invited to find a way towards peace and reconciliation.

# Panther

Element: **fire**
Season: **winter**
Keywords: **abandonment, solitude, healing wounds**

Panthers possess great inner strength, the kind that allows them to be happy when they are alone with themselves. If you encounter its energy the panther invites you to process your wounds related to abandonment, whether they are symbolic or real. Learning to appreciate moments of solitude will help you learn to love yourself and no longer fear silence.

## MESSAGES

The panther has come to help you heal an old wound. A feeling, insecurity or abandonment may have been conditioning your relationships with others as well as your self-image. You are much stronger than you think, so recover your self-confidence as you have all the potential you need.

### Relationships

*If you are in a relationship*: an abandonment wound can make you dependent on your partner. This form of compensation unbalances your relationship and can weigh on the person you're with, who may feel invaded and deprived of a part of their personal freedom.

*If you are single*: healing an abandonment wound or at the very least becoming aware of it will ensure that you will not attract people who would only deepen that wound.

### Work

An abandonment wound impacts your investment in your work, and you suffer from low self-confidence. You have a tendency to do more than is asked of you because you need your management's approval to feel validated, yet this tactic does not yield the hoped-for outcome and results in a deterioration of your self-image. The panther urges you to believe in yourself more.

### Family

It is most likely that your feeling of abandonment is directly related to your childhood, but it may also have been passed down to you by a family member who experienced this trauma. A heart-to-heart discussion on this issue could provide some answers and give you greater strength and self-confidence.

### Health

Abandonment wounds have a direct impact on your self-esteem, and therefore on the way you take care of yourself. Don't neglect yourself. Take the example of the panther, which has no fear of displaying its vitality and breathtaking beauty.

## SPECIAL MESSAGES

**If you dream of a panther**
You have incredible potential just waiting to be expressed if you can only release your fears related to abandonment.

# Parrot

Element: **air**
Season: **summer**
Keywords: **cultural diversity, sharing**

Parrots open you up to a world of colour and diversity. With their gift for speaking they invite you to communicate in other languages, with other cultures and with the globalisation of the world, remembering that the richness of this sharing comes from your ability to open yourself up to others.

## MESSAGES

You are never too old to learn a foreign language or to perfect your knowledge of one. Languages are a real asset when travelling and exploring the richness of humanity in each country. The colourful parrot knows that happiness awaits you if you make an effort to open yourself up to other cultures.

### Relationships

*If you are in a relationship*: cultural differences can sometimes be problematic in your relationship. Your education and points of view can differ and cause misunderstandings, but beyond these conflicts your story is uniquely rich.

*If you are single*: you are attracted to difference, and you are quite right! Don't be afraid to be unique and seek out the exotic, as you could find yourself enchanted by a foreigner.

### Work

Opening your work to other countries could be a good idea. You are invited to go towards new international collaborations or partnerships, so don't be afraid to travel to educate yourself.

### Family

Ethnic diversity in a family is a source of enrichment. Whether you come from a different background or are the first person in your family to initiate that diversity, be aware of the positive thing it brings your clan: a great breath of fresh air in everyone's habits!

### Health

Travel broadens the mind, but this can also be applied to mental health. Seeing the world pushes you to put the smaller worries of your daily life into greater perspective and tune in to the present more. Open yourself up to the world and other cultures for greater freedom of thought.

## SPECIAL MESSAGES

### If you see a parrot
A trip abroad is in the works. Brush up on your vocabulary, as you will soon be called to practise a foreign language.

### If you own a parrot
You like diversity, and this openness towards other cultures is an asset. You need colour and exotic things in your life to avoid boredom.

### If you dream of a parrot
You could learn a lot about yourself if you explored other cultures.

# Peacock

Element: **spirit**
Season: **spring**
Keywords: **beauty, creativity, artistic vision**

Peacocks enchant with their beauty, speaking of rainbows and colours mixing and fanning out. These birds can seem superficial until you start to look beyond their appearance. The peacock helps you develop your creativity, and with its support everything will be an explosion of colour, wonder and magic. Each hue has its own significance and natural expression, as the peacock embodies the palette of possibilities on earth.

## MESSAGES

Seeing the world through the eyes of an artist isn't a sign of eccentricity, but rather means that you are able to capture the magic of colours in nature through a rainbow, sunrise, flower or bird. Everything is there right before your eyes for your enchantment. Your sensitivity enables you to connect with these energies related to colour. The peacock invites you to consciously observe nature to find deep nourishment.

### Relationships
*If you are in a relationship*: just like the colour of a room impacts your mood, your relationship emits a frequency that could be perceived as a colour. Each couple resonates with its own colour, and the union of both your energies creates this unique frequency.

*If you are single*: attraction is visual but it also happens on an energy level. If you choose a partner for their beauty you run the risk of missing someone with a heart full of love.

## Work

Some people like to show off, their ego concealing how poor they are inside, while others know that there is another truth. The peacock will help you thwart the pitfalls of superficial relationships so you can have more confidence that you are in the right place.

## Family

You are very talented, a gift you have inherited from your family. This part of you is just waiting to be more fully expressed, and your view of the world is supported by your ancestors' blessing.

## Health

You are asked to love your body as it is with all its imperfections as all forms of beauty have their place on earth. Reveal your own and take ownership of its uniqueness!

## SPECIAL MESSAGES

### If you see a peacock

Don't focus on your physical appearance but on your personality, your soul. Be willing to embrace every aspect of yourself. If the peacock is fanning out its tail feathers it means that you know how to see the beauty in all things, beyond appearances. This path nourishes your creativity, so keep exploring it.

# Pelican

Element: **water**
Season: **winter**
Keywords: **poetry, sensitivity, beauty**

Pelicans are among the biggest birds with the capacity to fly. Graceful and skilled at fishing, they have a yin or feminine energy that is emphasised by the fact that they live close to water. The pelican is an ally if you are opening yourself up to your sensitive nature and working towards greater self-knowledge.

## MESSAGE

The pelican invites you to dive into your inner world of poetry and sensitivity. The rush of emotion you feel at the beauty of nature will enable you to truly discover your ability to listen to your sensitivity. The more you accept that part of yourself and give it room the more it will show you the way forward.

# Pheasant

Element: **fire**

Season: **summer**

Keywords: **royal couple, twin flames, karmic ties**

Pheasants represent the royal couple, the union that exists between two souls who desire to experience a physical and spiritual fusion. Connected with the element of fire, the pheasant resonates with twin flames who find each other again in this life, helping them to heal their relationship and transform the fire of passion into a less destructive form of love. When the pheasant appears to you it means that something has already been integrated and assimilated inside you. You are ready to move into the dimension of the pheasant!

## MESSAGES

Love is complicated, and experiencing a tumultuous relationship can be a source of deep questioning. When love destroys more than it builds, what is the purpose of the connection? The pheasant wants to help you enter into a healthy relationship, be it with your current partner or with someone else. You will be able to transform your relationships by becoming aware of what you are coming back to experience on a karmic level, which is concerned with twin flames.

### Relationships

*If you are in a relationship*: the pheasant speaks of love, of course, but first and foremost it is trying to show you the sacred part of this love: the depths of your connection. You already knew your partner in another life, which explains your complicity but also the difficulties you sometimes experience together.

*If you are single*: you have been scorched by a former love and are nursing a few burnt fingers. The pheasant invites you to free yourself from your karmic ties with that person, as they could trouble your future relationships. You are urged to meet again to heal, see the healing process through to the end and open your heart up to more peaceful relationships.

## Work

Try to avoid mixing work and love, which rarely ends up well and especially when there are unresolved karmic ties. You run the risk of finding yourself in a complicated situation.

## Family

Your family may completely disapprove of your relationship with your twin flame, a relationship that seems chaotic and painful in the eyes of your loved ones. They care for you and want you to be happy, so don't hold it against them. The love you are experiencing is complex and they haven't necessarily encountered it in their own lives, so show them that you will grow from this relationship. The pheasant has come to help you heal the flames of the past.

## Health

A relationship with a twin flame isn't exactly restful and is putting a serious strain on your heart. You may be showing signs of weakness, because your body is revealing the limits that must not be crossed in this relationship. The most important thing is to have respect for yourself. Sometimes the healing process can lead to a separation, especially when your body communicates that it's at the end of its rope.

### If you see a pheasant alone

Your karmic past is still influencing your love life. Give yourself permission to freely move towards a more peaceful relationship.

### If you see a pair of pheasants

You are capable of helping your relationship evolve towards greater exchange and sharing.

### If you find a pheasant feather

Your romantic past is about to resurface.

# Pig

Element: **earth**

Season: **autumn**

Keywords: **happiness, kindness, hedonism**

All kindness and bonhomie, pigs love the good things in life and have emancipated themselves from the rules of propriety. Contrary to a hygienist and right-thinking nature, this animal loves to take a roll in the mud. Perhaps the pig can teach you to find happiness in simplicity and in a less conventional way than usual?

## MESSAGES

Eating with your fingers, jumping in puddles and dancing in the rain: indulging in childhood pleasures can be a lot of fun! Stop being careful not to get dirty and live simply with the elements of nature. Children know how to do this naturally but are conditioned from the earliest age to conform to the rules of propriety. How can you find that way again as an adult? Let your inner child refresh your memory.

### Relationships

*If you are in a relationship*: little mannerisms are charming, but in the long run they can be difficult to endure for your partner. If you have a tendency towards fastidiousness or a lack of flexibility you can adapt your personal organisation from time to time to make room for improvisation and a touch of folly.

# P

*If you are single*: the pig's motto is that the simple, good things in life are worth experiencing. Enjoy! Don't deny yourself the pleasure of a meal or outing with someone you like, as it will do you the world of good.

## Work

The workplace is often governed by propriety. Having the boldness to move out of the usual conventional framework requires a lot of self-confidence and courage, yet many people hope that this will change and just wait for someone to pave the way for them. Think about it the next time you feel judged.

## Family

If you have children or grandchildren or if you think you will have them one day, take a leaf out of the pig's book and break free from useless codes of morality. Jumping in puddles when you are well protected from the rain has never hurt anyone! There are so many 'good' standards we can afford to transgress sometimes to better appreciate the little joys in life.

## Health

What do a few extra kilos matter if you are happy that way and accept your body as it is? Those kilos are less harmful to you than a succession of useless diets. Enjoying life does not mean doing things to excess, but allowing yourself small indulgences and embracing them fully without feeling guilty about them.

## SPECIAL MESSAGES

### If you dream of a pig
Plan for a few changes in your usual day to day life. Try to break your routine a little to invite new things into your life.

## If you see a pig

A part of you yearns to dance under the rain but another, more conventional side of you prevents this. Why not let the first part take the reins once in a while and have a little fun?

# Pigeon

Element: **spirit**
Season: **autumn**
Keywords: **forgiveness, love, direction**

Pigeons possess an energy that invites you to forgive yourself for the mistakes of the past and others for their weaknesses. Forgiveness is a powerful loving force that allows you to see life from a different angle and identify how to guide yourself on your path. Pigeons are capable of finding their way back from hundreds of kilometres away. The pigeon comes to help you find the way of forgiveness if you are lost in resentment.

## MESSAGES

You have set aside the past, thinking that would help you find your way forward, but this effect only lasts for so long. The pigeon invites you to dig out what you have buried and examine it in the light of the present moment. What are you able to forgive? Can you observe that situation from a different angle and show yourself greater leniency?

### Relationships

*If you are in a relationship*: instead of chewing on old resentments, wipe the slate clean and give yourself permission to start anew on solid foundations. Forgiveness is essential if you want your relationship to last. If some things are impossible to forgive your happiness will be hindered in the future.

*If you are single*: do you still feel resentful towards former partners? Think about it, and forgive yourself for your errors in judgement. Life wants to take you on new paths, and there is no need to take the past along with you. Give life a chance to prove to you that something else is possible.

## Work

You are exacting and often set very high standards for yourself. Be willing to accept that to err is human and that your life isn't at stake. Forgive yourself for your weaknesses and fatigue, because you will see that you will feel much better if you put less pressure on yourself.

## Family

You don't choose your family and yours can sometimes drive you mad, but nobody's perfect! Whether it's towards a loved one or yourself, don't stay fixated on your resentment. Life is short and regrets stay with you, so try to forgive before it's too late.

## Health

You are well grounded, which enables you to always reconnect with your energy centre. Love is your main drive, so become aware of the strength this emotion can bring you as it will make you climb mountains.

## SPECIAL MESSAGES

### If you see a pigeon

You need to stop obsessing. Take a moment to be still and let negative thoughts leave your mind, then you will see how they become less important as they gradually disappear. Through this, reconnect with your strength of character and an ability to see things in a more neutral way. Your judgement will be clear and objective, free of polluting emotions.

### If you have pigeons around your home

Forgiveness is a strength, a very powerful force of love that you can use daily to make your way forward. If that force is not yet active in your life, let it show you an incredible new path.

### If you find a dead pigeon

The past needs to be released, because resentment is preventing your heart chakra from opening up. Let go of the old to make room for the new.

# Pike

Element: **water**

Season: **winter**

Keywords: **tenacity, boldness, strength**

Pikes are carnivorous fish reputed for being extremely voracious, but in fact they only attack when they have a particular goal in mind: to eat. Outside this particular circumstance pikes are really quite placid animals. They don't eat when they're not hungry, contrary to what stories may say, but their tenacity makes them formidable predators and they won't hesitate to use their strength to attack bigger fish. Pikes are also water guardians that regulate aquatic energies.

## MESSAGES

There is no point in fighting like crazy; it is better to wait for a real opportunity. The pike has come to you to warn you that a situation is going to need all your boldness and strength, and that you will have the capacity to be victorious as long as you hold on to your goal.

### Relationships:

*If you are in a relationship*: a rival is circling around your partner, so you are going to have to bare your teeth to safeguard your relationship. Know how to preserve what matters to you.

*If you are single*: competition can sometimes be fierce on the single-people market. If you have someone in mind, give yourself the means to win over this person.

### Work

The pike urges you to show more ambition and not give up. You can attain your goal, and your tenacity will be your biggest strength!

### Family

Sort through your relations and protect the people you love from toxic relationships. This cleansing may be crucial to restoring inner calm and the peace of quiet waters.

### Health

Your determination and mental strength have a positive effect on your health. Still, don't forget to fully enjoy the calmer moments between more hectic times. In this way you will be able to recharge your batteries.

## SPECIAL MESSAGES

### If you catch a pike

Your ambition sometimes puts too much pressure on you. Start by listening to your heart, and only after that follow your ambitious energy and not the reverse.

### If you see a pike in a river

You are encouraged to go further in your life, to put your energy at the service of a greater goal. You have the shoulders for bigger responsibilities.

### If you dream of a pike

Tenacity means knowing how to use your energy over time. Don't hesitate to take a break now and then to recharge your energy for more efficient action.

## FINDING NEW STRENGTH

The spirit of the pike came to visit me in a dream one night. It wanted to feed on the flesh of my calf and I was trying to avoid it by climbing up a ladder in the water, but the pike kept coming back. In the dream I wasn't afraid for my body as I felt the pike wasn't trying to harm me but to communicate a message through its determination. When I woke up I felt that the pike had come to give me strength to see my projects to the end.

# Praying mantis

Element: **air**

Season: **summer**

Keywords: **inner harmony, sacred feminine and masculine, magic**

Praying mantises are discreet animals that rarely appear before humans. The females are well known for their voracity towards the males, and their energy is a combination of yin, with their delicate and elegant appearance, and yang, as evidenced by their strength. The praying mantis invites you to find a happy medium and balance within yourself so you don't succumb to inner power struggles.

## MESSAGES

You can sometimes be excessive and behave impulsively, and your relationships with people may be coloured by power struggles. For better emotional balance you need to bring your inner feminine and masculine energies into harmony. The praying mantis has come to help you maintain healthy and harmonious relationships.

### Relationships

*If you are in a relationship*: the praying mantis invites you to take stock of your place and your partner's in your relationship. If something is vexing you, try to find a positive means of expression to avoid a power struggle. Everything begins with inner balance. Do you give your inner masculine or feminine side enough space to allow that balance?

*If you are single*: before thinking about meeting someone, perhaps you should connect with your inner self. Make peace with the opposite sex, heal your past wounds and bring your masculine and feminine sides into harmony. In a cosmic dimension, your future romantic relationship will be all the more sacred for it.

## Work

Praying mantises are solitary creatures. Perhaps you should take off for a while to get started on a project. Take care to set aside some time for yourself in your work, as it is important to take breaks away from your team so you can restore your energy.

## Family

The praying mantis is the fairy of magical moments. This power animal will often pay a visit during family meals or parties to help you keep these precious memories with you.

## Health

Your vitality depends on your capacity to be alone and maintain healthy relationships. If there are too many conflicts around you, find a way to develop inner harmony. If you are in an agitated environment, give your body what it needs to calm down and recharge its energy.

## SPECIAL MESSAGES

### If you see a praying mantis perched on a plant

The praying mantis invites you to observe the way you operate. Do you feel more yin or yang? What place can you give each of these parts inside you?

### If you see a praying mantis in flight

Enjoy the magical energy of the present moment. There is something precious there, so seize this opportunity!

**If a praying mantis comes into your home**

You need to engage in some personal work to reconnect with a masculine or feminine part of yourself. The praying mantis will bring you the path of balance.

## A MAGICAL MOMENT OF ENCOURAGEMENT

We were having an impromptu dinner among friends, a simple but authentic moment. We were celebrating life and the hope that our friend would fight and overcome a new cancer that, after many examinations, appeared to be curable. A praying mantis arrived, flying around us many times to show us its fairy wings and release its present-moment magic.

# Rabbit

## (and hare)

Element: **earth**

Season: **spring**

Keywords: **time, growing old, life stages**

Rabbits are swift, agile creatures, and with them everything happens very quickly. The rabbit speaks of your relationship with time that flies by too swiftly and helps you release your anxiety about growing old or fear of entering a new stage in your life. The rabbit comes to support you in your important life transitions.

## MESSAGES

You are at the dawn of a change in your life, and you may be feeling fear in relation to time passing by. Growing old and moving into a new life phase are not easy things to accept, so you need to show yourself some leniency so the important transitions can occur in stages. The notion of time slipping through your fingers only exists in your head, and time can become your ally if you enjoy every step of the way. There is no need to project too far ahead in time.

### Relationships

*If you are in a relationship*: the rabbit speaks of descendants and legacy. You may be moving towards having a baby, seeing one of your children leave the nest or becoming a grandparent. Take time to talk it over with your partner, especially if you are feeling some anxiety about it. You need time to adapt to major life changes.

*If you are single*: romantic relationships are a stressful topic for you, and you may sometimes feel that other people judge you for being single. There is no need to be so anxious! Feel free to follow your own path, because if you labour to meet your loved ones' expectations you could end up making the wrong choices.

## Work

You have a never-ending to-do list to manage, feel increasingly pressured and are anxious about the possibility of not reaching your goal. Emergencies can't always be your only drive: you need to be able to take breaks in your everyday life and take back the reins of your time.

## Family

Leaving childhood and entering your teens is an important stage of life, the time during which you as a child psychologically separates from your parents to move towards individual thinking. This may have been a difficult phase for you, which would explain why you have feelings of anxiety or doubt at each major stage in your life. Think back to your choices and your parents' reactions: were you allowed to go against the established order?

## Health

Constant stress in your body will weaken your health. You need to find ways to bring your cortisol levels back down to strengthen your immune system. Identify the causes of your nervousness: the answer is often hidden in the problem itself!

## DIFFERENCES BETWEEN THE RABBIT AND THE HARE

The rabbit comes to help you accept that time passes and support you in letting go of your fear of growing old. The hare has stronger energy, pushing you to jump forward without wasting time.

### If you see a rabbit

Pointless stress causes anxiety and tires out your body. Repeat the following mantra when you expect too much of yourself 'I am . . . . . . enough.' (Fill in the blank according to the circumstance.)

### If you see many rabbits at once

You feel slightly overwhelmed by a situation, so take a step back before diving into action or be more patient. Don't put so much pressure on yourself.

### If you see a hare

If a question is going through your mind, here is the answer: 'The time is right!'

# Raccoon

Element: **water**

Season: **winter**

Keywords: **sense of touch, hand healing, magnetism**

Raccoons dip their food into water before eating it, and in some languages their name reflects that habit. They have very sensitive and mobile hands and possess an extraordinary sense of touch. Their eyesight, however, is rather underdeveloped. The raccoon will appear if you are in need of using the energy in your hands for healing. Magnetism is a wonderful tool, and the raccoon invites you to explore it further.

## MESSAGES

You have a lot of magnetism in you, with an ability to alleviate pain through the use of your hands. If you are still unaware of your gift it may be an opportunity to explore it. Humans have a tendency to neglect their sense of touch, preferring to focus on their other senses. The raccoon invites you to take an interest in that particular sensitivity.

### Relationships

*If you are in a relationship*: in time people in a relationship can become more distant with each other. The raccoon urges you to reconnect with physical touch that is not of a sexual nature, and increase the time you spend together with greater tenderness.

# R

*If you are single*: all humans need to be touched, kissed and hugged for their well-being. It is perfectly normal to want to have someone in your life who would give you these things, so ask the universe to bring a benevolent partner onto your path.

## Work

Your magnetism may be reflected by your natural charisma. You capture people's attention, and you know how to use this to your best advantage. Keep cultivating positive thoughts to attract collaborators who will vibe on the same energy level as you.

## Family

You have received from your ancestors a talent for healing with your hands. Seek advice from the people around you who use this ability to alleviate pain, which will help you call upon your gift and explore it further.

## Health

Your skin accumulates information throughout the day. A massage would help you release tensions and other emotional loads and reconnect you with your body and physical sensations.

## SPECIAL MESSAGES

### If you dream of a raccoon
You will soon receive an opportunity to experiment with the magnetism in your hands.

### If you see a raccoon
You have a gift for healing and alleviating pain through your hands.

# Rat
## (and coypu)

Element: **earth**
Season: **winter**
Keywords: **survival, intelligence, cunning**

Rats are capable of surviving in any environment. Their intelligence is individual as well as collective, as they concern themselves with their own survival but also that of the group. They are determined creatures and never let go of anything. Rats learn in ways that enable them to defy traps set by humans, and their cunning endows them with a slightly provocative spirit.

## MESSAGES

The rat invites you to examine the part of you that lives in survival mode. In what area of your life – relationships, money, food – do you have a tendency to function as though you were afraid of lacking? That fear of scarcity was passed down to you by a group such as your family or another collective. What do you need to let go of to enjoy life with a lighter heart?

### Relationships

*If you are in a relationship*: you know how to use your charm to get your partner to do what you want. Take care not to go too far, though, or it might backfire on you.

*If you are single*: there is a family memory inside you, a voice that seems to say, 'I'll manage better on my own.' That memory is most probably connected with trauma or complicated romantic relationships in your family line. If you were to deactivate that survival mode, what would be your true desires?

### Work

You often fret about your income and ability to bring in enough money to support your family. Release your fear of scarcity, as your intelligence will always enable you to find sources of income.

### Family

Your ancestors have handed down to you a heavy past filled with memories of scarcity. Your job right now is to release these fears so you can defuse the survival mode that permeates your cells.

### Health

There is a fear of illness in your family history. You need to understand that although you may have inherited genetic predispositions to certain diseases, their activation largely depends on your environment and state of mind.

## DIFFERENCES BETWEEN THE RAT AND THE COYPU

Coypus are essentially water dwellers. They help you release emotions related to your place in society, while the rat concerns itself with issues of survival. The coypu is a rather positive power animal that wants to show you how it manages to carve out its place in an environment full of other species. Your difference is not an obstacle to your fulfilment; on the contrary, you will turn it into a strength for you have the talent to make your own way.

## SPECIAL MESSAGES

### If you see a rat in the street

Everything that doesn't belong to your inner world appears as a threat from which you must escape. You are invited to drop your weapons so you can find peace.

### If a wild rat comes into your home

You are encouraged to defuse fears related to scarcity. The group is paramount to you, so trust in the people around you more so you are able to let go.

### If you have a domestic rat in your home

You like to go against the current of society, which you take wicked pleasure in defying. Your independent nature sometimes baffles your family, so take care not to isolate yourself too much as you do need others in your life.

### If you find a dead rat

Take stock of your fears related to scarcity and ask the dead rat to help you release family memories for greater self-confidence. Thank the dead rat for its help.

# Raven

Element: **spirit**
Season: **autumn**
Keywords: **magic, parallel dimensions, states of consciousness**

Ravens guard the gateways to other worlds. They live in dimensions parallel to yours, and appear in the here and now to show you this magical path. Ravens hold the key to your altered states of consciousness and watch over your spirit when you embark on journeys of the soul. They bring you back safely, making sure that all your parts are reunited correctly before you come out of the altered state and back into your usual awareness.

## MESSAGES

Your dreams carry messages that your mind is not yet ready to contemplate in real life. The raven tells you that these dreams are also soul journeys, and that it has come to make sure everything goes well. Take note of your dreams, as they contain truths for you to explore.

### Relationships

*If you are in a relationship*: love is like a great journey, crossed with unknown paths. The raven has come to tell you that you are not yet done discovering your partner, that they have parts of light in them waiting to be revealed. Don't fall asleep in your day to day: go on an adventure.

*If you are single*: certain fantasies or dreams are keeping you in a false reality, which may result in disappointment and frustration in your encounters with people. Put yourself in alignment with your reality so that what you are seeking can present itself to you.

## Work

You are beginning to realise the impact you can have on the world when your consciousness opens up. This new outlook on yourself will lead you to rethink your work environment. Bring change into it to make it look like the person you are becoming.

## Family

Take stock of the people who regularly appear in your dreams, as this likely holds a message for you.

## Health

You are made up of many energy bodies, and this multidimensionality is beginning to take shape in your mind. The more you become aware of the impact that energies and the unperceived have on your body the more you will resound with your full potential.

## SPECIAL MESSAGES

### If you hear a raven caw

Think of your last dream, as it deserves to be recounted to someone who will be able to help you decode it. If the dream is about a particular person, perhaps they are the one to whom you should speak.

### If you see a raven walking around

You are attached to a reality that brings you reassurance. Don't be afraid to leave your comfort zone, as your grounding is strong enough to keep you from getting lost.

### If you see a raven taking flight

Your thoughts are seeds of creation. Which ones are on your mind in the instant you see the raven take flight? Thank the raven for helping you become aware of what you are creating. If necessary, you can correct your state of mind by starting a more positive inner dialogue.

## If you see a flock of ravens

An important dream might come to guide you. So you can embrace it, try not to eat too much before going to bed and turn the lights off early as your chances of entering into a sleep phase conducive to lucid dreams will be better. Set an intention before going to sleep and leave a notepad and pen near your bed so you can record the particulars of your dream when you wake up.

## If you find a dead raven

An inner world of yours is currently changing completely that might be a karmic memory rising to the surface of your awareness so you can be released. Pay attention to the signs that will reveal to you what that memory is. The raven has come to help you clear the past.

## If you adopt a raven

You are one of those people who know that there are many different planes of reality, and you travel between realms with ease and subtlety. The raven is your ally to help others see the world with fresh eyes.

# Red kite

Element: **air**

Season: **autumn**

Keywords: **precision, perfectionism, letting go**

Red kites are birds of prey with a keen sense of detail, and their sharp eyes enable them to see small things from a high altitude. The red kite is an ally if you are a perfectionist who is particularly demanding in your work, and will help you be ready to take the plunge even if you are not sure of finishing your task.

## MESSAGES

Your perfectionism is an immense asset, but it is also the main obstacle to your personal fulfilment. At times your quest for quality prevents you from entering the arena, but if you spend too much time in thinking and preparation then you will never dive in. It is time to use your skills as they are and perfect them along the way. The hour has come to spread your wings and take flight!

### Relationships

*If you are in a relationship*: if you are pushing back a decision from fear of making a mistake, the red kite has come to reassure you. No one is ever 100 per cent sure they will  spend the rest of their lives with someone. Be bold, and commit fully to a path with your partner.

*If you are single*: you are very demanding of yourself, which has an impact on others. Before judging someone, start by accepting your flaws and weaknesses as a part of who you are, as this will enable you to better accept someone else's vulnerability. They will then be able to reveal their inner beauty. Imperfection deserves to be loved.

## Work

For you work is a source of pleasure because you like to give things your all. Still, you need to compromise with your perfectionist nature to allow yourself a little spontaneity along with your rigour. Don't let your attention focus on the details; instead, maintain an open mind to fully experience each stage of your progress.

## Family

Your ability to go into every detail is something you have inherited from your family, and you know how much of a challenge that quality is. You should nurture your need for optimal results, but don't forget to compromise with others to show them kindness. Sometimes it only takes a short step to turn an artist into a tyrant, so learn to accept the mistakes of others and stay on the path of tolerance.

## Health

By forcing yourself to reach certain goals you put yourself under a lot of pressure. This can be harmful to your health, because you can push your luck too far. You are allowed to be tired, and you are allowed not to make it every day. Repeat these words to be more indulgent towards yourself and bring some flexibility into your exercise routine.

## SPECIAL MESSAGES

### If you see a red kite sitting still

Sometimes it's when you let go that you can open your mind and see things with greater clarity. You will be more efficient if your mind is rested, so take breaks in your work or take time to think about a project.

**If you see a red kite in flight**
Let go, and stop being so demanding of yourself. Remember that no one is perfect and be willing to accept your flaws.

**If you find a red kite's feather**
Let your artistic sensitivity show you the middle way between work and pleasure.

## LETTING THE MAGIC OPERATE

I love animal photography. On one occasion I had gone up into the mountains searching for birds of prey when I saw a flock of red kites in a field. Rather than just one or two individuals, I had around 20 of them to photograph! I had no choice but to set aside my perfectionist nature if I wanted the magic to operate, and I was able to take many photos while still enjoying this moment of close proximity with the kites. When I arrived home one picture really stood out from the rest, as though the kite was offering itself to my lens. In the end, because I had been willing to simply enjoy the experience that had been sent my way I was able to take a picture I was entirely satisfied with.

# Rhinoceros

Element: **earth**
Season: **winter**
Keywords: **deep intuition, telluric forces, listening**

With their horns, rhinoceri pick up on telluric forces, or those that arise from the earth. They feel and perceive their environment through a wavelength located on their third eye. The rhino speaks of deep intuition and special ties to the elements, especially the element of earth. This power animal listens to its environment because it is in that space that all answers can be found.

## MESSAGES

You can trust your intuition. If you have questions on a particular place where you live or would like to live, know that you are in the right place when you feel your heart aligned with what you want. There is no need to rush, as the answers you need will come to you at the opportune moment.

### Relationships

*If you are in a relationship*: the rhinoceros listens, feeling the earth and its answers. What do you feel when you truly listen to your partner? See how truth lies in simple things.

*If you are single*: the magic in meeting someone also rests on following your feelings and intuition. Don't let your fears related to past experiences derail what you deeply perceive. True love is right before your eyes.

### Work

Rhinos only charge when they feel threatened. If you feel there are tensions or rivalries in your workplace, don't let that disturb you because your energy, supported by the rhino, will enable you to avoid external attacks.

### Family

Your empathy and capacity for listening mean that you are able to help others accurately. For even greater efficiency, wait for people to come to you for help. You will lose less energy because those people will be truly ready to receive your assistance.

### Health

Your third eye chakra, which enables you to see beyond appearances, is opening up and connecting with your soul. Some interference is possible because your vibratory rate is in full motion. In the event of headaches, connect with the earth so you can release them.

## SPECIAL MESSAGES

### If you dream that you encounter a rhinoceros

The rhino helps you become aware of the change in your vibratory rate. Support this inner movement by connecting with your new frequency.

### If you dream that you are attacked by a rhinoceros

You are fighting a part of yourself, that part of you inside that knows the truth. Your mind is still trying to gain precedence over your intuition, so have confidence in yourself!

# Robin

Element: **air**
Season: **summer**
Keywords: **simplicity, laughter, carefreeness**

The robin comes to awaken your cheerful inner child, the one that used to love to run after butterflies and grasshoppers and laugh without a care in the world just because life was beautiful. The robin invites you to bring lightheartedness and simplicity into your heart and taste the uncomplicated beauty of the present moment.

## MESSAGES

Look back in time to remember your inner child and a cheerful memory from childhood, such as a moment of joy perhaps with an animal or in nature. Let that sensation rise up in you like a wave of lightheartedness and playfulness and flood the present moment.

### Relationships

*If you are in a relationship*: why should a relationship have to rhyme with monotony and habits? Indulge in suggesting simple moments of togetherness such as a board game that could spark laughter and feelings of closeness. There is no need to look far, as everything is at your fingertips. Use your child's imagination.

*If you are single*: there is no point trying to control and anticipate everything, as life takes care of bringing the right people onto your path when you're ready. Be open and sociable and unafraid of meeting people, and leave room for spontaneity.

## Work

Don't check your inner child at the door when you enter your workplace. Let it come in with you, as it will bring a dose of lightness and fun into your day. Don't forget that a mischievous child hides behind each of your collaborators, and exploring how to connect with those inner children is excellent for bringing new ways of communicating into your work environment.

## Family

Not everyone has had a joyful and happy childhood, but every child has the ability to dream and escape through their imagination. Ask your loved ones to tell you what they dreamed of, as you might be surprised!

## Health

Laughter is the medicine of the soul. If you nurture your sense of humour you will be able to navigate difficult situations with greater detachment and a better perspective. Don't let yourself be completely engulfed by dark thoughts; see how you can keep a little of your child's heart alive.

## SPECIAL MESSAGES

### If you see a robin
Your day is filled with cheerful energy, so let that vibe flood your heart.

### If a robin has decided to live in your garden
You are in the process of letting positive energies related to childhood rise to the surface of your life. The robin will support you in reconnecting with your imagination and playfulness.

### If you find a dead robin
A wound from your childhood needs to be healed so you can recover your capacity to laugh at life's difficulties.

# Rooster

Element: **earth**
Season: **summer**
Keywords: **self-esteem, success, pride**

Roosters are leaders: without them, a coop just isn't the same. Their pride is unequalled and they love to parade around, show off and crow. In a way roosters are crooners for their ladies. Their ego leads them to not doubt themselves for a second, and through their attitude they can kindle feelings of esteem in others and become their worthy representative. The rooster will appear to you if you lack self-confidence or don't dare to shine and accept your success.

## MESSAGES

The archetype of the egotistical leader strutting around is preventing you from accessing a more positive version of yourself, suggested by the rooster. It is up to you to reinvent what it means to be a leader. If you don't accept the idea of achievement you will never shine, so release negative thoughts associated with success and dare to become an inspiring model for others.

### Relationships

*If you are in a relationship*: you like to seduce and charm. Despite being loved by your partner, you need reassurance from other people. Don't go too far, as this attitude could get you into trouble with your partner.

*If you are single*: you are at the height of your powers of seduction and like to feel that it is easy for you to obtain what you want. On a deeper level this game enables you to avoid potential suffering, so become aware of this so that a deeper romantic relationship can become possible.

## Work

You are so talented, and by recognising this fact you will be able to contemplate your success as a natural process without any ego or misplaced pride. Achievement does not necessarily mean rising above other people. Stay true to yourself and acknowledge your success, as it is a source of inspiration for others.

## Family

Strong personalities certainly aren't few and far between in your home! Family meals sometimes turn into rounds of cockfighting, with you as a participant. You need to temper that particular trait and turn it into an asset so you can stand out among others. Let your voice be heard.

## Health

You need to get it out of your head that success is in some way a negative. First and foremost, success is a form of recognition for your work, for who you are. If you don't take your rightful place your energy will diminish along with your self-confidence. Acknowledge your talent, and you will be at the height of your motivation.

## SPECIAL MESSAGES

### If you hear a rooster crow
The time has come to acknowledge your ability to be in the spotlight. You are a spokesperson.

### If you see a rooster
You are one of those people who have something to pass on. Release any negative feelings about leaders and take your rightful place.

# Salamander

Element: **fire**
Season: **summer**
Keywords: **creation, materialisation**

Salamanders are connected with the earth's fire and specifically the fire of lava. The salamander is at the beginning of all project creation and materialisation. This power animal makes innermost thoughts possible and grounds them in earthly reality, helping you if you are a dreamer to turn your ideas into concrete achievements.

## MESSAGES

There is no ideal age or situation to dive into a project that can be born of a desire, need or thought: whatever! The salamander wants you to be proud of yourself and finally dare to bring your project to life with the help of your inner fire, the one that guides your actions. The salamander will help you make a dream come true.

### Relationships

*If you are in a relationship*: if you want to build something together, be it a trip, house or family, you need to give yourself the means to do it. Even if it takes time, the salamander will help you persevere and manifest your dreams.

*If you are single*: whether you're dreaming of living with someone or alone, nothing will happen if you don't get a move on. The salamander has come to help you make destiny happen!

## Work

Set yourself concrete goals to see your project through. Start by talking about it to get help from people who will be able to advise and assist you in identifying the key steps. No task is too heavy to handle if you break it down into smaller pieces with the idea of bringing the overall project to life.

## Family

Your loved ones are not necessarily the first people to validate your ideas, because in doing so they might have to accept that they never gave themselves the means to go through with their own. However, it can be liberating to follow your instinct, to show yourself that you can give life to any idea with enough effort. With some time and a little perspective your efforts could even help others dare to make the leap themselves.

## Health

Your creative fire could lead to problems with your joints or inflammation issues if it is not channelled in a positive direction. Don't try to smother that fire, because in the end it will burn you up from inside. You would do better to make more room for it.

## SPECIAL MESSAGES

### If you see a salamander in the water

You know how to temper your inner fire by channelling your emotions without losing sight of your goal. Keep creating new things; it is a mission of yours on earth!

### If you see a salamander out of the water

You are looking for your path, the meaning of why you incarnated on earth. You want to leave a trace of your passage here, and you largely have the means to do so if you make an effort to materialise your ideas.

# Salmon

Element: **water**
Season: **spring**
Keywords: **loyalty, sacrifice, goals**

Each year salmon swim back up the rivers where they were born to reproduce and lay their eggs. Once their task is done they die of exhaustion. The salmon's strength and determination enable it to reach its goals. This power animal also embodies loyalty and complete sacrifice for the benefit of its line and species. Its energy is related to family memories, and it underlines the impact these memories can have on your life.

## MESSAGE

You are going against the flow to the point of exhaustion. What are you trying to do? Who are you trying to please? Could your state of fatigue be hiding a duty of loyalty towards your clan? Like the salmon you make every sacrifice to reach your goal, but is that goal really yours? Staying on this same path comes with such a cost of effort when it would be so much easier if you let yourself be carried by the flow.

# Scarab beetle

Element: **spirit**
Season: **winter**
Keywords: **afterlife, the deceased, rebirth**

Scarab beetles have connections with the afterlife, their spirit moving between life and death. This power animal knows the importance of cycles and accompanies souls to the other side. In return, these souls can ask the scarab beetle to carry messages of hope back to their loved ones.

## MESSAGES

You have recently lost a person or animal you loved, and the scarab beetle appears before you to communicate their message of love. Rebirth is at the heart of the scarab's thoughts, because it knows that life and death are intimately intertwined. Have faith in life and in the presence of your loved ones beside you, and embrace this message of love.

### Relationships

*If you are in a relationship*: a deceased person is watching over your relationship. That person is giving you their blessing and will protect your love so it may always remain intact.

*If you are single*: a deceased person is guiding you to meet someone. You are going to receive signs from the universe, so pay attention!

### Work

Your spirit guides know your skills and values and want to help you see yourself in a positive light. You are going to receive messages from them that will help you develop greater self-confidence.

### Family

Your family members who have passed on are sending you signs. You are invited to receive their love from the other side and understand that they never abandoned you. They love you and want to prove it to you.

### Health

Grieving is a complex process and can sometimes be a long one. Abandonment wounds are just as difficult to release, as they follow you in every aspect of your life. Embracing the scarab beetle's message will give you an opportunity to move forward in greater peace once a loved one has left you and receive the love they can still give you.

## SPECIAL MESSAGES

### If you see a scarab beetle

A deceased person or animal is sending you a message of love and peace from the other side, informing you that their spirit has been released into the light.

### If you see a dung beetle

Dung beetles recycle dung from other animals. The dung beetle is a messenger of rebirth and invites you to be willing to let go of your negative thoughts so you can transcend the passing of a person or animal you loved. Guilt has never made anyone come back from the dead.

### If you find a scarab beetle in your house

Someone you were close to is sending you a message of love from the other side. Life goes on, and that person would like you to be able to feel joy free from guilt.

## A SIGN FROM THE OTHER SIDE

Not long after the death of our cat, Rumba, we went to the forest for some fresh air. There were scarab beetles everywhere, hundreds of them. As I was caught up in the moment I was unable to receive the message intended for me, for it often happens that I find meaning in a situation once I am able to take a step back from it. When we got home a dried golden beetle was waiting for us in the middle of my dining room. This sign was a message from Rumba, announcing her upcoming reincarnation. I embraced this message of her release and all the love she was sending us like a gift.

# Scorpion

Element: **fire**
Season: **summer**
Keywords: **life force, resistance**

Scorpions vibe with brilliant, burning energy, their life force providing them with prodigious resistance. They possess a very active defence mechanism, and will appear to you if you are in need of reconnection with your primary nature so you can face a person or situation that is putting you in danger. The scorpion's fire is like a flamethrower ready to be released any second, but those who know its true strength only use it when absolutely necessary.

## MESSAGES

Waste no more time with harmful people or toxic situations: take flight or fight when you find yourself in danger. If the scorpion appears to you it may be because you need to reconnect with this primal instinct. If you think too much you will forget to take action, so you need to consider a radical solution.

### Relationships

*If you are in a relationship*: if your relationship is going through a stormy time, distance yourself from it for a little while to take stock. Channel your inner fire and impulsive nature to make the right decisions.

*If you are single*: a wound from the past still burns too strongly to let you engage in a new relationship. Appreciate this time alone as an opportunity to reconnect with yourself and become aware of your strength.

### Work

The workplace sometimes requires you to bare your teeth. The scorpion is not one to be pushed around, so if you are attacked in some way set your boundaries so you can be respected.

### Family

Scorpions are solitary creatures, but don't forget to stay in touch with your loved ones. Don't isolate yourself too much, or you might reinforce your defensive nature. Confide in people you trust so you can defuse the tensions inside you.

### Health

All that fire burning inside you is connected with your vital strength. As long as you maintain a balance in your life you will have a lot of energy, but in the event of difficulties or conflicts that fire will backfire on you and become harmful to your digestive system and liver. In this environment of organic stress you run the risk of developing kidney stones.

## SPECIAL MESSAGES

**If you see a scorpion**

It is time to put an end to a situation or conflict. It is crucial, actually non-negotiable, for you to take action so you can find freedom. This is the mantra of the scorpion.

**If you dream of a scorpion**

Your mind burns with brilliant fire, a fire that carries extraordinary energy as long as you channel and orient it towards constructive projects. Don't waste your time feeling resentful or engaging in incessant conflicts.

# Seagull

Element: **water**

Season: **winter**

Keywords: **strong character, cleansing, circle of life**

Seagulls generally live close to the sea but they can also be observed in great numbers in cities, where they find a profusion of waste. Seagulls are among the cleansers of the ocean and are more or less appreciated due to their grouchy personality. They know how to make room for themselves with the help of loud shrieks if necessary.

## MESSAGES

What if you were to give yourself permission to say 'No'? What boundaries would you like to set in your life? Look at the seagull, unafraid to displease and daring to take its rightful place and oust the competition. To survive you sometimes needs to elbow your way through and seize opportunities as they come, which is what the seagull has come to teach you. Some chances only come along once, and if you want to seize yours you will have to be ready.

### Relationships

*If you are in a relationship*: the seagull speaks of boundaries. You may need to redefine yours more clearly so you don't find yourself carping all the time. If something doesn't work for you don't let the situation deteriorate, but instead put a firm framework in place.

*If you are single*: your strong character can frighten a potential partner away. You may need to water down your wine a little if you want to attract someone, but don't give up on showing your true colours or flaws so you can feel comfortable in your encounters. People need to see you and take you as you are.

## Work

Your grumbling tendencies can irritate your colleagues, so try to be more positive in your everyday and express yourself with greater diplomacy and then you will gain in better leadership. You have the strength of mind needed to take the lead as long as you soften the edges of your temper.

## Family

You will only be able to live in harmony with your family once you manage to see the glass as being half full. Every situation deserves to be analysed from more than one angle. Stop acting like a child and become an adult, then you will see that you want for nothing. Everything is within your reach.

## Health

When you don't assert your heart-felt choices with sufficient strength you will end up in stressful situations. Everything starts with you, so stop playing the victim and take steps forward while listening to your inner voice. You have the capacity to move mountains.

## SPECIAL MESSAGES

**If you see a seagull in town**
An opportunity is about to present itself, so pay attention!

**If you see a seagull near the sea or the ocean**
Your temperament is mellowing as the years go by and you are gaining in maturity. Keep listening to your inner voice.

### If you hear a seagull squawking

You need to say 'No' or set the required boundaries. Take action instead of griping.

### If you find a seagull feather

Don't be afraid to assert yourself.

### If seagull droppings land on you

You are advised to change your way of seeing things, because by adopting a new point of view you will see that everything isn't all that bad. To address a situation you need to be aware of all its positive and negative aspects. Take a global view of it, as that is how you will find the best solution.

# Seahorse

Element: **water**

Season: **autumn**

Keywords: **paternal energy, freedom from patriarchy, masculine sensitivity**

Seahorses are also known as hippocampi. The female transfers her eggs into the male's belly, and the dad to be keeps them warm until they are ready to hatch. The males are therefore the ones to give birth to the young in this species, an exception to the rule in the animal kingdom, so the seahorse thus sheds light on a father's role. Through its energy and presence on earth this power animal frees men from years of patriarchy that have prevented fathers from showing their true capacity to care for their children.

## MESSAGES

The seahorse has come to help you contribute to rethinking the role of men in society. Men and women are all responsible for the evolution of the world we live in, and men can now openly take ownership of their sensitivity and paternal fibre. It is incumbent on all of us to work towards this transition, because the children of tomorrow need fathers who are actively engaged in their education.

### Relationships

*If you are in a relationship*: the manner in which children are educated conditions how they will behave as adults. You are naturally supposed to identify with your parents' model, but you are under no obligation to do things like them. On the contrary, don't shut yourself up in stereotypes as you must be free to express your sensitivity.

*If you are single*: you cannot find fulfilment in stereotypes of the past. You want to change established codes, and your future partner will be of the same mindset.

## Work

Your place at work should depend on your skills and never on your gender. You can help mindsets evolve towards greater equity and are invited to actively engage in this noble cause.

## Family

Some patterns in the education you received will have led you to rebel against the established order and social injustice, and respect for women is of particular importance to you. Sexism creeps in at the earliest age, so educating children differently is the main way to bring change into society.

## Health

Your sensitivity and sense of justice can sometimes cause sparks to fly. If you feel particularly strongly about something not much is needed for your blood to boil, but anger risks putting a serious strain on your body by weakening your liver functions. Digestion is your sore spot.

## SPECIAL MESSAGES

### If you dream of a seahorse
You have the power to bring mindsets to evolve. You are invited to become active in favour of greater equality within society.

### If you find a dried seahorse
A memory tied to a sensitive man in your family who was misunderstood and suffered for it still influences your everyday life. In light of this information you need to reconsider the place of men in your life.

## If you see a seahorse

Passing your values down to your children is a key to releasing ancestral memories connected with the place of men and women in society.

# Seal

Element: **water**
Season: **autumn**
Keywords: **creative process, comfort zone, rest**

Seals aren't very comfortable on dry land, yet they need to leave the water to give birth. The seal teaches you that it is necessary to move out of your comfort zone to create. The creative process requires first and foremost a rested and open mind but also for you to venture into different worlds, and often involves putting yourself in a little danger. It is through that vulnerability that seals can be observed. If they never ventured onto solid ground you would never catch sight of them, and the same goes for your ideas. You are invited to display them and take action!

## MESSAGES

Something is preventing you from making your way forward, and there is a huge step to be taken between your thoughts and the reality of your life. You would like to show what you are capable of doing, but for that you need to leave the water and display your creations. The seal encourages you to take risks, as that is how you will be able to bring a desire to life.

### Relationships

*If you are in a relationship*: move out of your routine and engage in new activities together. Make an effort to leave your comfort zone, because you might be surprised.

*If you are single*: habits are reassuring and give you a sense of security. Could you perhaps unwittingly be stuck in a rut? Would you be capable of changing if you met someone?

## Work

Bring novelty into your work life. You can move out of your routine by changing jobs, developing new skills or even changing the decor in your office. Get yourself moving: that is what the seal is inviting you to do.

## Family

Breathe creativity into your family environment, the space in which you find the greatest fulfilment. Let your yearnings run wild, as they will bring balance into your life.

## Health

A healthy mind in a healthy body is an adage you would do well to heed. Take time to rest so you can think more clearly. A walk in the forest or a lovely bath would do you the world of good.

## SPECIAL MESSAGES

### If you see a seal

To see a creative process through you need to move out of your comfort zone. Be bold and venture beyond your usual world.

# Shark

Element: **water**
Season: **winter**
Keywords: **barriers, passages, boundaries**

The energy of the shark speaks of the past and the future. It comes to help you take important steps to move to another level, a process halfway between fear and a rite of passage. The shark reminds you that it is sometimes good to experience milestone events so you can break free from old limitations. Growing involves being willing to make leaps forward.

## MESSAGES

Your greatest stumbling blocks are the ones you set yourself. The shark wants to help you go beyond what you think you are capable of doing or being. Fear is also an excellent signpost, as it indicates that a door is opening before you.

### Relationships

*If you are in a relationship*: your relationship needs to be taken to a new level. There is a project that you are not implementing out of fear of commitment, and you are invited to overcome that obstructing fear. Your fears are only founded on old, mistaken ways of thinking, so it is time to align with your future.

*If you are single*: if you don't make a huge effort to move forward you run the risk of living eternally in the past.

## Work

Why are sharks associated with money-hungry people? Perhaps a shark is only someone who pursues a goal without ever letting go. If you were hoping for a promotion, go after it! It won't turn you into a grasping person.

## Family

You need a securing framework to grow, but then you need to learn to leave it and make your own way. It seems you may not have yet reached the end of this stage, as you don't feel authorised to pursue your own path. Don't wait to be validated by your family to do what you think is right, because you are a responsible person and need take ownership of your choices.

## Health

Many moments in life can be rites of passage, such as passing the threshold from life to death but also many other landmark events. When you are willing to move forward and grow you also become willing to grow old. Don't be afraid of time: it does take you forward but you won't enjoy life more by ignoring it.

## SPECIAL MESSAGES

### If you dream of a shark

An initiatory experience is in the works and will probably reveal itself to be a major leap forward. Consider whether your fear is guiding you towards what deserves to move in your life.

### If you see a shark

Release any limitations that no longer serve you. You hold the reins of your life and are responsible for your choices.

# Slug

Element: **earth**

Season: **spring**

Keywords: **vulnerability, soul families, true nature**

Slugs, unprotected by any shell, give an impression of vulnerability, yet they possess incredible resistance. Their strength comes from their ties to the group and their ability to work collectively. Slugs are connected with their soul families and work with their peers for the survival of their species. Their ability to live without a carapace invites you to release any filters behind which you hide to avoid showing yourself in your true, authentic light.

## MESSAGES

You yearn to resonate with your true nature in the world, yet a belief along the lines of 'If I reveal myself as I truly am I will be vulnerable' persists inside you. The slug wants to show you that, on the contrary, in doing so you will be recognised by your peers and your soul family and you will all be able to work together. How can a true meeting with them happen if they don't see you?

### Relationships

*If you are in a relationship*: you and your partner belong to the same soul family. In the presence of your partner you are able to remove your carapace and be yourself. Don't you wish to feel that confidence and have that authenticity in your everyday life? Think about what you would gain if you lived without filters.

*If you are single*: soul families are destined to meet and recognise each other, as long as the right signals are sent out. If you hide behind a protective barrier no one will be able to see you. Be yourself, and you will attract the right person.

## Work

Your work environment sometimes requires you to act under cover, to put on a mask and take on a role that has been pre-established for you. You may then be overcome by a feeling of deception, making you feel as though you have lost your identity. The slug wants you to think about how you could show yourself to others in a more authentic way. Do you really need that mask? What does it protect you from?

## Family

Vibing in harmony with your loved ones goes far beyond your line. The slug invites you to connect with the great all, with the universe, as it is through that global connection that you will find the belonging you yearn for.

## Health

When you make your way forward with an open heart you are aligned in your thinking, and you resonate with who you really are and are comfortable in your body. The slug has no need for a shell. Think about why that is: is it because it has too much self-confidence, or because as it feels no fear it has no need to take refuge in a carapace?

## SPECIAL MESSAGES

### If you see a slug

You can take off your mask and let go of your role playing, and move into greater authenticity with yourself. This won't make you more vulnerable, as true strength lies in self-confidence.

### If slugs take up residence in your vegetable garden

A protective barrier is preventing you from having the boldness to leave your shell. Slugs invading your vegetable patch isn't an attack launched against you. If you hear their message they will go away. 'Leave your comfort zone and move out into the open, unprotected,' is what they want you to hear. 'Be authentic in the world, as exceptional encounters are in the works for you.'

### If you see a great many slugs

You are currently connecting with humanity as a whole, which is immense and contains the souls of your heart family. Give thanks for this connection on an invisible level. You are all spinning a network of light.

# Snail

Element: **water**

Season: **autumn**

Keywords: **social norms, material needs, love**

Snails have no need for a place to live, as they are at home everywhere they go. Being hermaphroditic beings, they don't need partners of the opposite sex and they have no need for strong bones to create their shells. In other words, snails are animals that go against the usual rules. The snail encourages you to let go of material needs that don't serve you and desires that don't fill your heart, because the most important things are inside you wherever you are.

## MESSAGES

Need is the cornerstone of advertising, so marketers try to create a feeling of lack. This lack becomes a need that has to be filled, but once a purchase is made the sensation of emptiness comes back along with a feeling of need. The snail has come to teach you that in fact you require very little to live and are capable of adapting with much greater ease than you think. Even better, the more you release your material needs the more you can invest in what truly matters: love.

### Relationships

*If you are in a relationship*: what means more to you, a gift of great value or quality time spent with your partner and their love and attention, which are priceless? Sometimes true declarations of love translate into pure, altruistic gestures towards the other person, and it is in these moments that the depth of your relationship will reveal itself.

*If you are single*: we live in a world of glitter and illusion, yet searching for a durable relationship is a journey of truth. Finding an authentic partner who embodies sincere values sometimes amounts to looking for a needle in a haystack, but if you make an effort to look beyond the usual standards of beauty and fashion you will find true love.

## Work

Society says that career success can be measured by your job and the salary you earn, yet there are a thousand different ways to feel successful such as having free time, enjoying an activity that is meaningful to you, feeling useful in your job and working alongside people who share the same values as you. Don't forget that your salary does not condition the value of your job. What are your true needs?

## Family

The death of a loved one and questions of inheritance often bring to light what mattered most to you. Your true heritage is the love that was given and received, and the moments that were shared together.

## Health

Snails enjoy relatively good health, but their capacity for self-protection is another story. A snail's shell doesn't always have the expected effect and can easily be crushed. Snails know they have a limited lease on life and they know the value of good health, something money can't buy, so they don't waste their time with those who would harm them.

## SPECIAL MESSAGES

### If you see a snail with its shell
You need to drink more water, and more often. You can go without many things to survive, but water is not one of them.

### If you see a snail without its shell

Don't let yourself be distracted by false needs put forward by advertising. Know how to see what really matters for your happiness.

### If you accidentally crush a snail

Don't waste your time with people who don't share the same energy as you and whose intentions are doubtful. Life is short, so you might as well surround yourself with good people!

### If you find an empty snail shell

What matters most isn't material, so try to fill up your heart in the same way a snail fills up its shell. When you die, that's what will remain.

# Snake

## (and grass snake, viper)

Element: **earth**
Season: **winter**
Keywords: **healing, beliefs, innermost being**

Snakes are guardians of the lower worlds. They often have a bad reputation worldwide and in the collective unconscious, for they symbolise temptation, forbidden things and consequently evil, but in shamanistic cultures and many others snakes have powerful healing abilities. This power animal brings about deep inner transformations coming from your innermost being.

## MESSAGES

The snake has come to you as a bringer of change. Something is asleep inside you and is asking to find a way into your awareness. It may be about healing certain beliefs and giving yourself an opportunity to see things differently. You need to be willing to shed your old skin so you can broaden your views.

### Relationships

*If you are in a relationship*: the snake invites you to try the way of sacred relationships. In both of you, your masculine and feminine parts are seeking a new approach to your sexuality and looking for sharing in awareness and harmony.

*If you are single*: the snake suggests that you review your expectations. What beliefs do you have regarding the person you are waiting for that could be erroneous? Take stock and widen your selection criteria.

## Work

You are stuck in a way of thinking that is no longer in harmony with your inner path. The snake is trying to bring you out of your limitations, so take a step back and see what you would like to change because that is where the key to your transformation lies. Perhaps everything is already there inside you and you only need to give yourself permission to shed your old skin.

## Family

If you have children the snake has come to show you that you don't always act in alignment with your convictions, and that you let yourself be influenced by external opinions. Trust in yourself. If your question doesn't concern your children then the answer stays the same: right now, other people's opinions are taking precedence over your life principles. You are invited, like a snake, to weave in and out of all the criticism and make your own way. Follow what resonates inside you.

## Health

Healing is already accepted by your body and is just waiting to manifest in your reality. Give yourself permission to receive this grace. If your health doesn't improve the snake urges you to review the space you give your beliefs, so healing can take on spiritual meaning first before expressing itself physically. Healing also means releasing patterns of thought so you can find a path towards happiness in the ordeal you are going through.

## THE DIFFERENCE BETWEEN THE GARDEN SNAKE AND THE VIPER

Both garden snakes and vipers have healing powers. The viper protects you from malicious intent, while the garden snake is in an energy of light.

## SPECIAL MESSAGES

### If you find yourself face to face with a snake

You are ready to confront things, and a new reality will come alive inside you. You are facing choices that aren't all that difficult to make. The hardest part is behind you, and all you need to do now is shed your old skin.

### If you see a fleeing snake

You are afraid of the change occurring inside you and are pushing back a new reality. You are staying in the past out of fear of going towards the future. You can relax, as the snake will help you gently navigate this transformation.

### If you are attacked by a snake

Your thoughts are your own worst enemy, and it is chaotic in your mind. Find new confidence in your light and your lucky star. The snake is trying to get you to move and has come to shake you up so you can recover your footing.

### If you find a snake in your house

Healing or change are in the works, and the manifestation of that will be abrupt. Don't panic! It might involve a house move or a sudden opening of the mind. Your inner world is trying to communicate with you and the snake will guide you, so you can ask it for help.

## A LIFE CHANGE

Catherine's encounter with a snake changed her life. 'I was on the phone on my patio with my partner when I saw a snake slowly crawl down a wall and slip behind the garden shed. For me that appearance was significant, but my partner mockingly retorted that strange things were always happening to me. I now know that the snake had come to draw my attention to my declining relationship. Not long after its appearance I felt myself able to break up with this man and freely shine who I really am.'

# Sole

Element: **water**

Season: **summer**

Keywords: **law of attraction, intentions, protection**

Soles are a flat fish for which the art of camouflage holds no secrets. This power animal's energy is very protective: the shape of its body and the way its eyes are positioned on one side give it the ability to see predators coming without being seen. The sole teaches you to pay attention to harmful energies and protect yourself from them. Adopting the energy of the sole will enable you to remain invisible to those whose intentions are unhealthy, all the while remaining open to opportunities.

## MESSAGE

You attract what you vibe. The sole invites you to change frequencies so you can isolate yourself from toxic personalities. Deep at the bottom of your inner ocean no one can see you, but from this new point of view you can observe everything. The sole protects you through its invisible action. Keep in mind that the law of attraction can play out in your favour if you learn to understand how it works. Don't be a victim: enjoy life, and the energy of the sole will open new doors for you.

# Song thrush

Element: **air**
Season: **spring**
Keywords: **conviviality, cooking, friendship**

Song thrushes are connected with the pleasures of life, the joy of sharing and friendships. Knowing how to have fun with your loved ones is just as important as learning how to be alone, as it is by taking a step back that you can appreciate these moments of togetherness. Food is also at the heart of the song thrush's message; cooking is a gift you can offer the people you cherish.

## MESSAGE

You are missing people you love, so why don't you organise something like a meal together to see them again? Don't wait until it is too late to devise occasions for get-togethers: take the lead and contact the people you carry in your heart. Friendship is a precious thing.

# Spider

Element: **earth**
Season: **spring**
Keywords: **wisdom, connectedness, imaginary realms**

Spiders are gifted with great wisdom for those who are able to perceive their magic. They spin their webs in the material world to remind you that your thoughts and actions have consequences in real life. These webs are in the image of your world, connecting dots in the same way that living beings are interconnected. The spider likes to take you on journeys into the imaginary and invisible realms, and it is up to you to make the effort to see this power animal's inherent beauty.

## MESSAGES

If you could wield magic power upon your fellow humans what would you like to change? Did you know that you can move skilfully on the web of life and spin ties with the world to make people around you evolve? All of your thoughts and actions are connected with the rest of the world. From your dreams springs a parallel reality and from your fears are born deadly traps, so let your dreams inspire your creativity to spin your own web.

### Relationships

*If you are in a relationship*: your personal or family history has been marked by toxic relationships and you abhor finding yourself caught in someone else's web. You make every possible effort to maintain your independence, as it means so much to you. Listen to the voice that helps you move freely in healthy relationships, and ask your partner to respect your intimacy to give you the breathing space you need.

*If you are single*: pay attention to your warning signals, and don't dive into a new relationship without first checking your inner compass or you might find yourself caught in that person's net. Once you feel you have the all clear you can move forward confidently, although it is a good idea to maintain a level of mystery, not show your hand right away and take your time to observe your potential partner.

## Work

For you independence means freedom, and you cannot live with a boss breathing down your neck and scrutinising your every move. You like to be in a dominant position and in control of a situation, but it would be good for you to relax and let your creativity guide you towards your true path.

## Family

If you feel caught up in difficult family dynamics don't hesitate to ask the spider for help. The spider is in touch with your ancestors, maybe a grandmother or a great-grandfather there to help you, and will enable you to obtain assistance from the allies in your past.

## Health

A healthy soul in a healthy body is the spider's guiding message, inviting you to take care of your body as well as the thoughts that nourish that body. Bring your real and subtle foods into harmony to optimise your vitality.

## SPECIAL MESSAGES

### If you find a spider in your bedroom

Take care of yourself and your sleep, because your dreams reflect your thoughts. Before going to bed you can ask to receive messages through your dreams.

### If you find a spider in your home

Inner balance must be favoured. You need to spend some time alone to recharge your batteries, and it would also be good for you to better organise your schedule to allow yourself some breathing space. Sometimes, however, the opposite happens and you feel lonely and it weighs on you, in which case you need to go out to forge new relationships with people. Learn to discern what you need depending on the day.

### If you find a spider in your car

A journey is in the works, so why not take a weekend away for a change of scenery? Put your fears aside and allow yourself some folly, as it will make you feel alive.

### If a spider climbs up on you

An ancestor is trying to contact you. Don't panic: it's just a visit!

### If a spider surprises you

Fear is never helpful, so consider in which area of your life you don't allow yourself to be free and creative. Be bold, and move out of your comfort zone.

### If you see a spider's beautiful web

Beyond fear lies the true beauty in everything. If you continue to look for the truth behind appearances you will discover the treasure of life.

## A FEAR OF SPIDERS

Marie was doing a training course in animal communication. During a drumming meditation session a spider appeared above her head, then disappeared when she returned to her usual state at the end of the session. I told Marie about this apparition, and she confessed that she had a terrible fear of spiders. We then talked about fears in general. One month later she had made progress on the meaning of what that spider had come to tell her: it was about her past relationship with her mother, which had been toxic and invasive. We did another drumming meditation session and the same spider reappeared, but this time Marie was able to see it and express her gratitude to it. Since then she has lost all fear of spiders, and the spider has become her totem animal and helps her spin her dreams in real life.

# Squirrel

Element: **earth**
Season: **autumn**
Keywords: **opportunities, savings, anticipation**

Squirrels symbolise quick action, curiosity and anticipation, and the squirrel will appear to help you if you need to plan for the long term and learn to set money aside. This power animal is an ally for thrifty temperaments and knows how to seize opportunities to store up for the winter.

## MESSAGES

Money is a form of energy, and it needs to flow. You are invited to let the squirrel demonstrate that a little anticipation will allow you to prepare for leaner times. It may be time to start saving money regularly to bring a project to fruition or compensate a loss.

### Relationships

*If you are in a relationship*: money can be a source of conflict in a relationship. Whether or not you combine your resources or keep separate budgets, think about saving a little for the future. A long-term project wants to come to life.

*If you are single*: don't look for a partner according to their financial situation, as that is a bad option if you're searching for love. You need money to live, but it can damage relationships rather quickly. The same goes if you were thinking about using your affluence to attract someone, as your money could attract ill-intentioned people.

### Work

Before rushing into new projects think about how you can anticipate that change. Secure your baseline so you can avoid setbacks in the months to come.

### Family

Inheritance is often a source of conflict. If you have potential heirs in your inner circle, discuss the details of your estate as soon as possible and while you are still alive. It might seem morbid, but clarifying the situation will prevent future quarrels.

### Health

You always want to manage everything at once and are exhausting yourself. You have great energy, but you sometimes have trouble feeling where your limits are. Plan for days off so you can relax once in a while.

## SPECIAL MESSAGES

### If you see a squirrel

What state are your finances in? Think of a clear project you have set your heart on, like something you want to buy for yourself or a lovely trip, and be ready to make a few small sacrifices so you can reach your goal.

### If a squirrel comes near you

You may have some trouble managing your budget, and there is nothing wrong in asking for help to make ends meet. The squirrel encourages you to anticipate rather than living from one day to the next.

# Starfish

Element: **spirit**
Season: **winter**
Keywords: **bringing into harmony, structure, inner balance**

Starfish have ties with the five elements and are connected with everything on earth. Like antenna, starfish channel forces to enable their collaboration. The starfish will support you if you need to bring the various aspects of your life into harmony, and shows that you cannot over-invest in a particular area of your life without unbalancing the whole. The starfish's legs represent love, your social and spiritual lives, material aspects and health.

## MESSAGES

When faced with a problem you have a tendency to focus all your attention on it and neglect other areas. The starfish invites you to rethink your balance and nurture each and every aspect of your life, because then in the event of problems it will be easier for you to recover your inner harmony. You are connected with all things and can delve into your many resources to find solutions.

### Relationships

*If you are in a relationship*: your relationship is solid and you know how to lean on it when you are having problems, but don't be afraid to ask your friends and family for help so you don't place all the weight of support on your relationship.

*If you are single*: searching for a partner shouldn't become an obsession. To be healthy, this quest must not eclipse other activities that bring you pleasure. In the same way, your feeling of solitude cannot be remedied merely through the presence of a life partner.

## Work

Material issues aren't the most important thing. If you rethink things more globally you will be able to see what really matters to you. You'll probably have to make concessions in one way or another, so you might as well be in complete alignment with what your heart tells you.

## Family

Your family is the foundation of your own structure, initially through the education you received and the attention given to you by your parents. Depending on the standards passed down to you, you have a tendency to invest your energy in more or less certain areas of your life. The starfish invites you to widen your scope so you can give life to each of your aspirations. What are your priorities?

## Health

The starfish speaks of harmony. Your body is your vehicle in this world, and pushing it to excess is harmful to it. When you invest too much energy in an issue you disconnect from your body, which then sends you warning signals. Try not to think only with your head but also follow your feelings, because the stress created by your thoughts will lead you to overstep the limitations of your body. Take some rest when you feel the need.

## SPECIAL MESSAGES

### If you see a starfish in the sea or ocean

You have succeeded in investing your energy in the important aspects of your life and can feel a sense of peace taking root inside you. You are achieving a milestone.

### If you find a dead starfish

Take care not to overstep your physical limits due to an excess of obsessive thoughts cutting you off from your ability to call upon your other resources: psychological, material, interpersonal and spiritual. You are capable of overcoming any difficulty.

# Starling

Element: **air**

Season: **autumn**

Keywords: **collective intelligence, community, prayer**

Starlings use collective intelligence to go further together. We are always stronger together, and that is their message. When the starling appears to you it is to urge you to join forces with other people, because you will come up with interesting ideas together.

## MESSAGE

Contrary to animals, humans don't always make sufficient use of collective intelligence. Whether with people you know or others you don't know, the starling invites you to experiment with strength in numbers. Praying is one way of connecting with group strength, as are concerts, shows and soccer games. Find out how this collective energy can support you.

# Stick insect

Element: **earth**
Season: **spring**
Keywords: **ego, judgement, beauty**

Stick insects are discreet creatures that melt into the background. They invite you to set aside your ego and observe the beauty around you. The stick insect urges you to divest yourself of your tendency to constantly judge what is beautiful and what is ugly, which also makes you judge yourself and cuts you off from your intuition and receptiveness to nature.

## MESSAGES

You have fallen into a habit of submitting to prejudiced judgements. Beauty, for instance, depends on criteria dictated by culture and fashion. The stick insect invites you to release these preconceived notions: perhaps you could try to see the beauty in all things. To do this you will have to set aside your ego that knows and adopt the humble position of one who explores. Stop judging yourself, and take pleasure in living and feeling.

### Relationships

*If you are in a relationship*: you force yourself to abide by ways of living or doing things that can be too influenced by what others think of your habits. If you dared to break free from these judgements, how would you allow yourself to be in your relationship?

*If you are single*: the ways you judge yourself and others hinders the possibility of meeting someone. Beauty is only a construct, because true beauty lies in the meaning of things and in feelings and the joy of loving. Try to release your judgemental ways of thinking so you can welcome a beautiful person into your life.

## Work

Compassion, empathy and kindness are precious human qualities. You embody these values, so don't try to change in order to please. Remain true to yourself.

## Family

When you vibe with love you would like to convince the people around you that it is the best way of seeing things. However, you must accept that everyone has their own pace and that truth moves through the way of the heart. Trying to convince someone is a form of manipulation by your ego that knows. Try to adopt a humbler position and share your infectious zest for life with others. People will choose or not to open themselves up to your world.

## Health

You can end up exhausted if you try to please others. Beauty is subjective: look at nature and how it reveals a kind of beauty where sacredness makes life vibrant. Draw from this energy a desire to be happy while remaining true to yourself.

## SPECIAL MESSAGES

### If you see a stick insect

Your views on beauty could benefit from being stripped of standards and other subjective judgements. Be willing to be yourself, and you will feel greater lightness and well-being. You are a flower among flowers, and diversity is indispensable in nature.

**If you find a stick insect in your house**
Your inner being is full of wisdom and dreams of listening to the world around you. Take time to explore all things that live alongside you on earth and appreciate their true beauty.

## SEEING THE SACREDNESS IN ALL THINGS

As I was preparing my supplies for a training session on animal communication I found a tiny stick insect on my portable speaker. It explained that it wanted to accompany me, so I took it along in a little box to introduce it to my students. I am certain that those who were able to connect with the stick insect remember the vibrant message it gave us that day.

That message was: 'You needed to see me. No, I am not just some small stick. I vibe with my plant host and melt into it to become it. This is a marvellous capacity based on a need for survival, because for me to be seen is to be killed, as well as a humble attitude, for to survive I must not be seen. All ego has left me and I see the world with new eyes, which is why I have come here today. I invite you all to see the world as I see it, to appreciate the beauty of nature and feel a stronger connection. I hope you will learn to nourish your heart and make it richer through your encounters with animals, plants and humans, because from your resulting vibration a new humanity will be born: one that will be more aware, divested of any desire to live for itself and ready to celebrate life and see with new eyes the sacredness in all things.'

Element: **water**

Season: **summer**

Keywords: **taking flight, perfectionism, letting go**

Stingrays are like birds taking flight, the only difference being that they fly in the water. The stingray teaches you to let life flow, enjoy it and, most importantly, simplify it. As a human your perfectionist nature will often lead you to complicate things, put unnecessary pressure on yourself and forget to enjoy the ride. The stingray's energy comes to help you with your emotions and especially anxiety, which prevents you from grounding yourself in the present moment.

## MESSAGES

What would happen if you expected nothing more special from life than what it has to offer you now: wouldn't you enjoy each moment and opportunity more deeply? The stingray wants to help you let go, in the sense of accepting that everything is perfect in the present moment. Letting go does not mean you can no longer think, but that you should try to have fewer expectations and put less pressure on yourself.

### Relationships

*If you are in a relationship*: perfection is an illusion because no one is perfect, and that includes you and your partner. By wanting to change the person you're with you forget to enjoy the path you both share. Everyone has their flaws, and accepting your partner as they are is the greatest way to show your love for them.

*If you are single*: even if it's not easy, let yourself be carried by the flow. It is natural to want to control everything, but it is also impossible. As long as you put that kind of pressure on yourself and your destiny nothing can happen.

## Work

Planning things, thinking them out and organising them are all tasks that require a lot of energy. Don't forget to make make room for more pleasant moments in your day to relax.

## Family

You worry every day about the future of your loved ones and feel a need to help the people around you. It takes a real effort on your part to let experiences present themselves rather than anticipating them. Try to trust in life and let your loved ones make their own decisions.

## Health

An excess of anxiety and control can lead to stiffness and back pain because you put yourself under too much pressure. The stingray invites you to bring some flexibility into your body or mind. Give yourself permission to be imperfect!

## SPECIAL MESSAGES

### If you dream of a stingray

Show more flexibility in your everyday life. No one is perfect, so see what you can let go of to lighten your load.

### If you see a stingray

Don't worry about the future. Instead, live in the present moment as you are experiencing a magical encounter!

# Stork

Element: **spirit**
Season: **autumn**
Keywords: **creation, fertility, material world**

Storks possess a particular energy as though, nesting in high places or on rooftops, they lived in another dimension. Storks have long been associated with fertility and a mission to deliver babies. What they really deliver is the possibility to co-create with the universe in which they live. When the stork appears it is to bring and to give. Its energy can only be felt if you vibe on the same wavelength, beyond material things.

## MESSAGES

The stork invites you to find grounding in your reality. Although you operate differently from other people you do have your own universe to bring into the material world. The stork wants you to bring to life one of your ideas, like giving birth on earth to a baby from another world.

### Relationships

*If you are in a relationship*: you have your own way of seeing things, and it is pointless for you to try to be like others. On the contrary, you are an example for other people: thanks to you they learn that there are other ways of being in a relationship.

*If you are single*: the stork invites you to understand that you vibe on a different wavelength than other people, so that you may find someone like you. Accept this unusual side of yourself, as it is part of your charm.

## Work

Bringing to life an idea or project could help you distil who you are in this world and find a happy medium between your energy and reality. Creation would be a source of deep grounding for you.

## Family

Family is paramount to you and you devote a lot of time to taking care of your house, your comfy nest. If you want to have a baby, the stork has come to announce the good news you were hoping for. It also might be a sign that a new furry or feathery friend may soon join your household.

## Health

You are generally spared health problems, for your high energy creates a barrier against infection. However, your difficulty in grounding yourself in reality could cause some intestinal pain, so you need to find your happy medium.

## SPECIAL MESSAGES

### If you see a stork flying in the sky
A trip could help you find inspiration for your projects. Don't hesitate to explore other worlds.

### If you see a stork in its nest
It is in your home that you must build your reality. Make the changes you need to make your home mirror who you really are.

### If you find an empty stork nest
A project is in the works. Be patient, as it will soon reveal itself to you.

### If you find that a stork has made its nest on your roof
It is high time to spring into action! You will be helped by the energy of the stork to see your project through.

# Swallow

Element: **air**
Season: **spring**
Keywords: **revival, principles and values, choices of the heart**

Swallows arrive with spring, announcing the revival of nature and sparkling thoughts. With the swallow, full vitality returns to the energy of life, and ideas and desires are born everywhere it goes. Swallows build their nests in houses whose occupants live according to principles and values that the swallow wants to bring to life. This power animal comes to confirm the choices of your heart.

## MESSAGES

You are brimming with ideas, and sometimes your head is filled with chaos. You no longer know if you need to follow the thread of your yearnings or let them evaporate. The swallow has come to confirm that the time is right to follow your heart. What was going through your mind when you encountered the swallow has been validated by its appearance.

### Relationships

*If you are in a relationship*: a house move, renovation work on your home or a project to do with real estate is at the heart of your preoccupations. It's a good time to make your nest more comfortable.

*If you are single*: it's a time of renewal and you feel a desire to go out, which is an excellent thing as you won't meet anyone by staying cooped up inside! Take advantage of the swallow's energy and go for walks in places where it is easy to meet someone. The swallow has come to announce that magic is in the air.

## Work

You are careful to show respect to others and underline the value of their ideas. By working within a group you will promote positive collective energy. Keep going in that direction!

## Family

Your family has passed solid human values down to you. The swallow invites you to place these values at the heart of your life choices, as you have to be able to carry these qualities in all aspects of your life.

## Health

You are brimming with yearnings and have the energy you need to bring them to life. Go for it; don't let that wave pass you by. The time is right to invest your energy completely in your projects.

## SPECIAL MESSAGES

**If you see a swallow**
A choice you made from the heart is confirmed.

**If a swallow makes its nest around your house**
You should make more room for your emotions, as they are a gift. Don't tamp them down to fit a standard: let your emotions guide you towards your path of personal fulfilment.

## ADOPTING A NEW PUPPY

This is the story Mélanie told me about her experience with a swallow: 'As I was contemplating the possibility of adopting a puppy a swallow flew into my bedroom. It hovered in flight above me as I laid in bed, then went out again. That was the day my puppy, Ryzen, was born! The breeder thought – wrongly - that he wasn't the right dog for me, but other instances of synchronicity prompted me to follow my heart. Another bird came into the house at the exact moment I was looking at pictures of Ryzen's birth, and just before I brought him home a buzzard flew very low just above my car. Without all these signs Ryzen and I wouldn't have been brought together.'

# Swan

Element: **water**

Season: **spring**

Keywords: **destiny, family memories, liberation**

Swans remind us of the story of the ugly duckling, in which a black duckling becomes a gorgeous white swan. In matters of family history this figure is a key to releasing memories inherited from your ancestors. The swan is an ally if you are going the wrong way and trace your route through family ghosts. The swan's mission is to harness its whiteness and purity to transcend past traumas and release the impact these have on future generations.

## MESSAGES

You hold an important, although not the simplest, spot on your family tree. The weight of your ancestors' history has an impact on your capacity to be happy, and your soul has made the choice not to follow what was unconsciously expected of you. This refusal looks like a challenge thrown in the face of your ancestors, yet they only want each and every one of their descendants to take their destiny into their own hands and find their own happiness. It is this freedom, which they never allowed themselves to experience, that you can now offer them by being yourself. If you turn your back on the heritage of the past you will serve your clan.

### Relationships

*If you are in a relationship*: your choice of partner is a source of disagreement with your parents. You have followed your heart and not what was expected of you but have faith: it is exactly because you don't flow into the expected current that this impacts your family relationships. You are right to prioritise your happiness.

*If you are single*: take care to not reproduce existing family patterns. You can write your own story, and this might actually be your mission within your clan. You are invited to release repetitive cycles in your family.

### Work

Your career path can be driven by reason or passion and it doesn't matter which, because what counts is that this path is your own. You cannot find fulfilment if you make your choices not for yourself, but to please someone or prove something to a family member. Trust in your inner voice, as it will guide you. At the risk of disappointing others you might as well be loyal to yourself.

### Family

Your personal choices can be a source of misunderstanding and conflict if they do not follow your parents' expectations. However, a theory always needs a counter example, so take the opposite line of the established order and follow your own path. Your family will oppose this at the beginning because your choices force them to question their own paths, but after a while what you do will prove beneficial to everyone. This attitude will require courage and inner strength, which you have in spades!

### Health

Health problems could arise to express family memories that you are not to shoulder as your own. Your body will have a better chance of finding its balance again if you are willing to follow your own path without guilt. You could even be the healer of your clan!

## SPECIAL MESSAGES

### If you see a swan
Accept your role within your family line, as you are a key element of liberation.

### If you dream of a swan
You are going to be faced with a heart choice. You may disappoint others, but you are called to follow your instinct. The disappointment will be temporary and will fade away in time. You can step forward with confidence, as your decision will prove liberating on many levels.

# T

# Tiger

Element: **fire**
Season: **summer**
Keywords: **inner fire, anger, forgiveness**

Tigers are capable of turning the fire of anger into a fire of healing love. The tiger will appear when you are ready to consider forgiveness and enter into a dimension where reason is mastered by the power of love. The tiger lifts the veil on your subconscious, so with this power animal prepare yourself to discover who you are in a new light.

## MESSAGES

Have you ever wondered why some relationships are so complex? The tiger wants to show you that you sometimes project anger that does not actually belong to you. You are a profoundly good and gentle person but you sometimes feel misunderstood, so something needs to be released so you can reveal your true potential.

### Relationships

*If you are in a relationship*: non-violent communication would be a useful tool to help you express what sometimes makes you angry about your partner while still supporting a spirit of understanding between you. Don't wait to explode before saying what you want to say.

*If you are single*: forget the past and the harm that was done to you, because you need to forgive to move forward. The tiger is here to help you find that strength in yourself, then your anger will be able to turn into a constructive force.

## Work

You have forged an outer carapace to give an impression of greater strength, but in reality that carapace is preventing you from maintaining authentic relationships. Don't be afraid you show yourself in your true light, strong and fragile at the same time, as you will be all the more human for it.

## Family

There are people among your ancestors who need your forgiveness so they can move on in peace. Send loving thoughts to those who have suffered, but also to those who may have caused harm. Your role is to release the anger in your line, not carry its weight.

## Health

Anger impacts your immune system and liver. It would be a good idea for you to detox your body from time to time with the help of supplements, and to work on your emotions so you can accept them.

## SPECIAL MESSAGES

### If you dream of a tiger

There is a force in you, a great creative fire that needs to be expressed. Make room for your passions and yearnings.

### If you dream of being eaten by a tiger

You may be feeling guilty about the anger you carry inside you. The tiger wants to help you accept and express this emotion so it doesn't devour you from within. You are invited to speak your anger or record it, and watch what happens. Anger just needs to pass. There is no need to give it space, so learn to accompany it kindly towards the exit.

## A DECEASED GRANDFATHER'S VISIT

M was in the middle of a shamanic meditation session accompanied by drumming when I saw right beside her a weeping tiger. The tiger was sad because it couldn't be heard. It was M's grandfather, present in spirit and waiting to be released through forgiveness. This energy had been in M's aura for years and was causing difficulties in her relationships.

She became aware of the things she could give herself permission to release and found herself better able to understand her relationship with others. Her grandfather, finally soothed by forgiveness, left in peace towards the light.

# Tit

Element: **air**
Season: **winter**
Keywords: **perseverance, volition, courage**

Tits can be blue or black capped, and a few species live in gardens. These little birds have strong personalities and know how to assert themselves. When it comes to survival they are guided by their instincts, and their pretty appearance must not make you forget that tits know exactly what they want. The tit teaches you how to stay on course whatever the circumstances.

## MESSAGE

In a shallow world you can easily be duped by apparent success or a happy life posted on social media. Without meaning to, some people can even discourage you from pressing on. The tit has come to tell you to stay true to what you want, because where there's a will there's a way!

# Toad

Element: **water**
Season: **spring**
Keywords: **ugliness, inner beauty, release**

Toads don't try to be good looking; you might even say they have thrown on the most hideous costume they have. The toad invites you to look beyond what is seemingly ugly. This power animal will appear to you if you are in need of expressing your inner beauty by accepting your outer appearance. Norms and criteria may give rise to self-doubt, but the toad can help you demonstrate what you truly have to offer.

## MESSAGES

Your appearance may have been a problem in your life, and perhaps still is. Whatever the case, the toad wants to help you accept the way you look. True beauty only exists in the eyes of those who can see beyond social norms, and a heart's shining light only reveals itself to pure souls.

### Relationships

*If you are in a relationship*: your insecurities may have an impact on your relationship. Don't expect your partner to heal you of your self-image because that release work is up to you.

*If you are single*: attraction and alchemy between two people don't depend on body measurements or circumstances. True love emerges between two souls who recognise each other beyond appearances.

## Work

Don't hide away, but be bold and shine! If you believe in yourself you are capable of accomplishing what you set out to do. Your physical attitude and way of expressing yourself say a lot about you. Your body is your best tool for communication, because first and foremost it's the energy you send out that people perceive.

## Family

You have in all likelihood inherited your ancestors' point of view regarding your body. Some comments can leave traces forever, but it is time to release the past and reconnect with a healthier attitude about your appearance.

## Health

Balance begins when you accept yourself as you are. The toad knows that few people will find him handsome, but what does it matter? You only need one person to turn your life around, and that person is you! Loving who you are is the greatest gift you can give yourself. Everything else will follow, and your body will thank you.

## SPECIAL MESSAGES

### If you come across a toad

Release your full potential by making peace with your body. The truth is elsewhere. Your energy is the first thing people see.

### If you dream of a toad

You are becoming a more confident person. You can leave your insecurities behind you and live more freely, aligned with who you are.

### If you see a toad that has been run over by a car

Don't let anyone judge you on the basis of your appearance, and don't let others tread on your toes. The toad wants you to keep your head high.

# Tortoise/turtle

Element: **spirit**
Season: **summer**
Keywords: **vulnerability, masculine/feminine duality**

Sheltered by their carapaces, tortoises feel protected from possible predators. Their energy is essentially yin or feminine, one of embrace and creation with the universe. Whether tortoise on land or turtle in the sea, this power animal is connected with the element of spirit and lives in another energy reality, one of original principal beyond masculine/feminine duality.

## MESSAGES

It is time to release the masculine/feminine dualities in you to let your feminine principal run wild. The creative process is connected with your ability to embrace thoughts and so you can manifest them on earth. It is time to let go of the carapace you have built that covers up your feeling of vulnerability. Let yourself be carried by the energy of the tortoise to co-create with the universe.

### Relationships

*If you are in a relationship*: the energy in your relationship stems from the energy you both carry. You are invited to enter into awareness of your relationship and release those dualities that only lead to conflict. It is pointless to take on a role that doesn't work for you. Remove your weighty carapace and find a happy medium to build together in greater harmony.

*If you are single*: your dual conception of the masculine and feminine needs to evolve so you can develop a wider conception of romantic relationships. Your own, inner relationship begins with you, by uniting your masculine and feminine energies. When that harmony is revealed you can move towards another kind of story, one made of love and sharing.

## Work

You have built a role for yourself, the one that was expected of you, and that carapace protects you from the outer world, which you find aggressive. Everything is fine; you have no need to feel vulnerable. The tortoise has come to announce a new era, one in which you will dare reveal yourself as you are.

## Family

Family relationships from one generation to another can be fraught with conflict, for you inherit a lot of resentment and unsaid things. You also learn to forge a protective shell against the toxic emotions of your elders and that shell is your ally, for it has protected you, but don't forget that it can also constitute an obstacle between you and the outer world. Release the resentment and unsaid things inside you to reconnect with your inner space.

## Health

If you don't give sufficient expression to your emotions out of fear they might explode, and they will block the flow of energy in your body and unbalance the hot and cold. Too much yang will lead to hot flashes, and an excess of yin will generate feelings of chilliness. See if your temperature regulates itself normally and, if necessary, find ways to bring it into better harmony.

## DIFFERENCES BETWEEN THE TORTOISE AND THE TURTLE

The tortoise is supported by the feminine principle and comes to help you go the distance you need to go to be able to see a situation more accurately. The turtle's energy is more yang or masculine. It invites you to release constraining thoughts so you can recover greater inner space and freedom of action.

## SPECIAL MESSAGES

### If you see a turtle
You are starting to emerge from a dual relationship so you can reconnect with the flow of life. Keep going in that direction.

### If you see a tortoise
You are not yet free to act as you would like because you carry a burden. Release the past, as it will give you a greater feeling of lightness.

# Trout

Element: **water**
Season: **spring**
Keywords: **sacred waters, memories, vitality**

Trout are attracted to pure, crystalline waters and are guardians of sacred waters, which purify you from the inside out. The coolness, clarity and sweetness of water are indispensable to the trout's well-being. The water you drink is just as important as the food you eat, containing nutritious elements but also positive memories and energies.

## MESSAGE

Pay attention to the quality of the water you drink, as water of lesser quality could be harmful to your vibratory rate. You are essentially made up of water, and each of your cells needs that element to thrive. You are invited to connect with water and its memories to become aware of its sacred nature. The trout wants you to purify your body with energised and vitalised water.

# Vulture

Element: **air**
Season: **spring**
Keywords: **cleansing, release, past**

Vultures are cleansers of nature, transforming all that is dead into life-sustaining nourishment. When the vulture appears it is to ground a change or idea, or help you move on to the next thing. The vulture will help you accept the release of what no longer serves you, and its ability to reach the skies gives it an awareness of what can nourish your soul. This power animal's teaching isn't necessarily gentle: when you need to take a band-aid off a wound to let it finish healing it's always best to rip it off in one go! The vulture helps you see more clearly into your past.

## MESSAGES

It is time to release the past and turn towards the future. A painful experience is in all likelihood preventing you from making your way forward, and the vulture wants to help you leap into the unknown and become aware of the important things you need to take with you in that jump. It would be pointless to burden yourself with cumbersome memories, so leave them in the past. The vulture is working to project you into the future.

### Relationships
*If you are in a relationship*: jealousy is never helpful. Your partner's past relationships need to stay in the past, so don't bring them into your story. To move towards the future together you need to learn to trust.

*If you are single*: fear of failure isn't getting you anywhere. Past mistakes belong to the realm of experience, so don't let them vibe or you might attract similar relationships. The vulture is urging you to visualise a beautiful encounter to make it come true. You are invited to become aware that your thoughts are at the root of a great many manifestations in your life.

## Work

Your lack of self-confidence can lead you to miss out on opportunities. There is no such thing as a perfect situation, so temper your tendency towards perfectionism and try out a few adventures brought to your doorstep by destiny. There are no risks except learning, as all experiences are in the end positive as long as they are accepted as such.

## Family

There are some family patterns that need to evolve, and you can help with this. Family habits can change if you really want them to. Communication can be made more mobile, for instance, emotions can be released or you can express your love for each other.

## Health

It may be time to let go of old habits and adopt healthier ones. It is never too late to start exercising again, change your eating habits, cut back on snacking and so on. The vulture will help you take care of yourself.

## SPECIAL MESSAGES

### If you see a vulture in flight
You are going to successfully heal an old wound and the vulture will help you turn the page.

### If you see a vulture on the ground
You will be able to bring change into your life when you become aware of the patterns still blocking you now.

V

## LEAVING THE PAST BEHIND

A participant in a meditation session was in the middle of a career change. She needed to release her past so she could move forward on her path, and the spirit of the vulture came to her. There are no such things as coincidences!

# Vulture, bearded

Element: **air**

Season: **winter**

Keywords: **nature conservation, way of life, cultural heritage**

Bearded vultures fly high in the sky and drop the bones they find on rocks to break them so they can pull them apart and feast on the marrow inside. This role as nature's cleaners is important in an ecosystem: the bearded vulture teaches you that every animal has its place in the food chain and that no one particular way of life can suit everyone. This power animal will appear to you when you doubt and question your cultural heritage on an ecological, environmental or societal level.

## MESSAGES

You are seeking your place within the human race and in terms of your consumer habits and impact on the planet. You are thinking in the right direction. You do need to accept that there are different ways of living and that you cannot change everyone, but you can live in a way that is aligned with your values.

### Relationships

*If you are in a relationship*: your differences in opinion as to how to adopt a more responsible way of consuming are a source of conflict. You cannot force someone to change: change must come from inside. Living under the same roof doesn't mean you both need to agree on everything, as everyone has their own pace.

*If you are single*: your values have taken an important place in your life and you're looking for someone who shares them. This is understandable, but it mustn't prevent you from keeping an open mind. Everyone can change and love can move mountains, so don't close the door on someone because of a difference. On the contrary: welcome this difference, because in our own ways we are all on one path.

### Work

You need your company to share your values and you need to feel in agreement with its purpose, yet the reality of things can sometimes be different and you feel guilty about staying in your job. Take things one step at a time to see what matters to you. Leaving a job or changing direction requires due consideration: do you imperatively need to leave now, or must you show a little more leniency for the moment?

### Family

Family members don't all have the same life purpose, which is why misunderstandings can arise. The important thing is to be tolerant; your opinions cannot take precedence over another's. Learn to respect each other in your disagreements, as your family balance is at stake.

### Health

Your body needs different things from other people's bodies. The more you listen to your yearnings the more you will allow your body to resound with full power. There are no general cases, so seek out your own singularity.

## SPECIAL MESSAGES

### If you see a bearded vulture

You are becoming aware of your place within the living world. Your desire to consider your impact on the planet is inspiring powerful reflections within you about the interdependence of species.

## If you dream of a bearded vulture

All dreams carry meaning and all humans have a purpose. Your purpose is connected with the cycle of life, the preservation of the planet and its animals, recycling and ecology.

# Weasel

## (and stone marten, ermine)

Element: **earth**

Season: **autumn**

Keywords: **lively wit, opportunities**

Weasels are playful, mischievous creatures that know how to discreetly take advantage of a situation. They prioritise comfort and will always be able to find a pleasant spot to rest in. The weasel will often appear if you are gifted with lively wit as well as strong hedonistic tendencies, and know how to bring situations to your advantage and enjoy life.

## MESSAGES

Life's pleasures are very often made up of opportunities to be seized at once. The universe is bringing you choices that will contribute to your personal comfort, and you are urged to accept them without guilt. After all, opportunities don't always present themselves twice.

### Relationships

*If you are in a relationship*: you have been dreaming of a comfy nest for a long time. Just like weasels know how to create their own dens using twigs, leaves and stones, use your imagination because treasures are everywhere. It is up to you to see and seize the opportunities around you.

*If you are single*: you are going to meet someone in a completely unexpected way, as though the universe had given a tap of its magic wand. You will have to react fast and accept what presents itself to you.

## Work

When you are motivated you're capable of displaying great energy. However, when you don't like a certain task you disappear off the map. You know better than anyone how to avoid being enrolled in a project you're not excited about.

## Family

Weasels love comfort and, above all, look to create warm and snug nests in which to welcome their young. Togetherness is very important to you, and you know how to host in style. You enjoy having loved ones around you at home for days on end.

## Health

You know how to take some rest when your body demands it. More importantly, you have a gift for accessing the good things in life, which makes you a lighthearted and enthusiastic person. The weasel supports your hedonistic side as a guarantee that you will remain in good physical and mental health.

## SPECIAL MESSAGES

### If you see a weasel

You are going to find something, maybe an old object, to restore. Don't be afraid to dive in, as you will create something beautiful. Go and grab your toolbox!

### If there is a weasel around your home

Your home is filled with cheerfulness and good manners; it is a happy place to live in. 'Welcome any stranger as a guest; they will leave when the weather clears' is the weasel's message for you. This power animal has come to support the welcoming and warm energy inside your home.

# Whale

Element: **water**
Season: **winter**
Keywords: **infinite love, memories, transmission**

Whales are among the biggest mammals on earth, and their energy is slow and gentle but powerful. They seem to evolve in another energy dimension, a realm of infinite flowing love. Whales carry the memories of the planet and are guardians of your inner depths, and they open and close the books of your soul and the doors of time. The wisdom of the whale extends far beyond your reality. To meet this power animal you will have to make an effort: forget the dual world and dive into an ocean of love.

## MESSAGES

The whale invites you to work for the greater good of humanity. What can you do to make the world of tomorrow more just and compassionate? You could simply reduce your waste or support local initiatives, or perhaps you wish to strive for something much greater. Whatever the scope of your action, make a start now as every step taken counts.

### Relationships

*If you are in a relationship*: the whale's message is that you shine, and this has an impact on other people. Your happiness is contagious and inspires others and gives them hope, so continue what you're doing to spread love around you. Love is your main drive towards joy.

*If you are single*: you have a big heart and believe in love at first sight, love that lasts forever, and you are right to believe. The whale will support you in your quest for true love.

## Work

Has anyone ever told you that you have a gift for transmission? You have a way of explaining things clearly and an ability to put people at ease. Your way of being will take you to new, uncharted territory. It would be a good idea to explore positions in management, tutoring, teaching and knowledge transmission, as these paths could bring you the purpose you are looking for in your career.

## Family

You ensure protection and mutual aid in your family, and it is often to you that people come with their secrets. So that this role does not become a burden you can ask the whale for help: the whale will lessen your responsibilities and help you recover more flow. You do not have to carry the weight of the world and should know that you are supported.

## Health

You are advised to preserve your body from the stress generated by your responsibilities. Your heart chakra will open up completely with the help of the whale and accumulated tensions will be released. You can use a visualisation meditation to cleanse your heart chakra.

## SPECIAL MESSAGES

### If you dream of a whale

An inner transformation is in progress. You have access to parts of your being that remained hidden until now. A door is opening towards a spiritual dimension that you need to bring into your reality.

### If you see a whale

You have just received a gift of infinite love, so open your heart and embrace it. If you read this message right after the encounter, close your eyes and relive the moment. The whale has opened the doors of time to you, and you can access its love far beyond your meeting.

### If you find a beached whale or see one on the news

Don't forget that you have a mission and are working for the world of tomorrow. The whale wants to remind you that the clock is ticking and it is time to dive into action.

## A DIMENSION OF INCREDIBLE LOVE

Just before a shamanic group meditation in the energy of the whale I channelled a message telling me to prepare a longer piece of music than the one I had initially selected. In fact, it took me more than half an hour to bring the participants, who were all experienced meditators, back into full awareness. Your encounters with the energy of the whale take place in the depths of your being, so to resurface from this journey and reconnect with the present moment your mind needs time. That day everyone agreed that they had felt as though they were in a dimension of incredible love.

# Wolf

Element: **spirit**
Season: **winter**
Keywords: **rightful place, clan, memories**

Wolves are pack animals that embody the notion of clan. The wolf invites you to reflect on both your soul and family lines, as though you could bridge them to find your rightful place. Every one of your actions is influenced by your karmic past as well as by the heritage passed down by your family. The wolf embodies, par excellence, the release of old patterns and will appear to help you learn to know yourself better and reveal your potential.

## MESSAGES

You are at a key time in your life, and certain choices and decisions will enable you take the place that is waiting for you. So you can make those choices in full awareness the wolf invites you to know yourself better. Who are you truly? Are your choices influenced by your karmic or family past? What can you release to relieve the weight of this position?

### Relationships

*If you are in a relationship*: do you feel that you are in your rightful place in your relationship? Are there any similarities with or differences from your parents' patterns? Examine anything you might be reproducing as though your freedom of action was hampered by unconscious

realities. Take a few deep breaths, close your eyes and visualise ties being undone, leaving room for your relationship to flourish.

*If you are single*: solitude and break-ups can be a result of personal choices, but they can also stem from memories from past lives or your ancestors' history. So that your choices can be as enlightened as possible, take time to meditate and visualise your heart being liberated to embrace love in all its forms.

## Work

In a wolf pack the alpha male guides the group but does not dominate others. In humans, that alpha male is the enlightened leader inside you and that part of you wants to be given more room and an energy of determination and confidence wants to express itself. Banish your doubts and move forward with confidence, as the wolf is with you.

## Family

Something is trying to emerge from the depths of your consciousness so you can liberate your clan. Being the person your ancestors were never able to freely embody is a wonderful gift to offer them. Be happy, as your ancestors are watching over you.

## Health

The state of your mental and psychological health depends in great part on what you have inherited from your ancestors, and on your conditioning and capacity to modify these genetic predispositions. Nothing is already written; you can shape your own destiny. The wolf invites you to take back the reins of your health.

## SPECIAL MESSAGES

### If you dream of a wolf

You are reconnecting with your personal power. Keep exploring your innermost being so you can discover who you really are.

## If a wolf attacks you in your dreams

There are memories in your past that need to be released. Don't be afraid of the wolf, as it is your ally when bringing memories to the surface of your awareness and helping you understand where the obstructions are coming from.

## If you see a wolf

You have already made good progress on your path and your place is well grounded. You know you can honour your ancestors and are aware of the strength they have passed down to you, as well as how far your soul has come.

# Woodlouse

Element: **earth**
Season: **spring**
Keywords: **ecology, responsibility, the earth**

Woodlice have survived for millions of years, almost without any change in their gene pool. Their energy is old, and they vibe with the earth's original frequency. Their close relationship with the plant realm teaches you to be humble and include yourself in a recycling process so you can minimise your impact on the planet.

## MESSAGE

What is the environmental footprint of your waste? Everything has an impact on the planet, and the woodlouse invites you to return to simple things and avoid as much as possible superfluous waste. The earth emits a benevolent, welcoming frequency and provides your sources of food. It is incumbent upon you to take care of the planet by giving due consideration to what you buy.

# Woodpecker, great spotted

Element: **air**

Season: **summer**

Keywords: **humility, keeper of history, plant wisdom**

Great spotted woodpeckers are guardians of forests and gardens that preserve dead wood from attacks by ravaging insects and watch over old trees. The great spotted woodpecker knows everything that happens in forests and accompanies people who take walks in the bush hoping to connect with the energy of that place. This discreet power animal will watch you and expect a humble attitude from you. Once it validates your presence it will guide you in your encounter with the plant world.

## MESSAGES

The great spotted woodpecker invites you to connect with old trees to receive the energy of the earth and wisdom of the plant world. The great spotted woodpecker is your ally when you are opening your heart to this energy. You are invited to learn to receive the magnetic fluid emitted by centuries-old trees, as they are the memories of the earth and guardians of the places they live. Take time to fully experience these encounters.

### Relationships

*If you are in a relationship*: the great spotted woodpecker is an ally for cleansing, renewal and reconnection with old values. Take time to look over your family albums and think about your ancestors, then share your story with your partner, children and grandchildren. Dive into those memories even if it means only keeping what matters to you.

*If you are single*: the great spotted woodpecker invites you to draw your family tree for the women of your line. Take time to think about what they experienced in their romantic relationships so you can sort through your family's stories and write your own story without repeating family cycles.

## Work

Take regular breaks near trees to release any negative energies you may have accumulated. Even if there are no trees around you, you can do a meditation or visualisation exercise. A wooden object can be a channel for connection.

## Family

Take time to listen to what your elders have to say while they are still here. Ask them to tell you about their past so you can pass on a duty of remembrance to future generations. Leave traces for others to find.

## Health

Take time to immerse yourself in the bush, which you need to recover your vital energy. Connecting with trees can help you bring your chakras into harmony.

## SPECIAL MESSAGES

### If you find a great spotted woodpecker's feather

There are good things and not-so-good things in everyone's life story, and what illuminates a path is a balance between the two. Remember to thank your ancestors for the gift of life they handed down to you.

**If you see a great spotted woodpecker in the forest**
Your inner demeanour is going to open doors before you. Stay humble, and you will be rewarded by the universe.

**If you see a great spotted woodpecker in your garden**
It's time to return to your roots, so organise a reunion with family members you haven't seen in a long time as it will recharge your energy.

# Woodpecker, green

Element: **spirit**
Season: **summer**
Keywords: **values, wood energy, spirit of ancestors**

Green woodpeckers are just as comfortable on land as they are in the skies. These birds embody the energy of a spirit connected with its ancestors and the balance between past and future. The green woodpecker teaches you that knowing where you came from enables you to understand where you want to go. This power animal knows that building your nest on solid foundations made of healthy wood requires time spent beforehand finding the right essence. The green woodpecker will help you spread your wings in full awareness.

## MESSAGES

You are on the verge of taking flight in a new way: through meeting your soul family! The green woodpecker opens doors that connect souls and enables them to find each other again. To support you in not losing touch with reality and your roots the green woodpecker will be at your side. Its wood energy will help you ground your spiritual experiences in the earthly world.

### Relationships

*If you are in a relationship*: meeting your partner was no coincidence. It's as though you were finding each other again, and this deep feeling has been with you ever since. The universe reunited you because you belong to the same soul family, and no words are needed for you to understand each other.

*If you are single*: it's time to walk through the door opened to you by the green woodpecker and meet someone belonging to your soul family. Your heart will set the pace for you and you will recognise the soul the universe sends your way.

## Work

Green woodpeckers are builders that don't wait for a nest to appear fully formed. They build their own havens, adapted to their needs. In relation to your work, this means that if you don't find a company to really suit you it may be time to create your own.

## Family

Your family has given you values and solid foundations that you can lean on to explore the subtle realms around you, and in particular the connections you may have with people from your soul family.

## Health

Your energy, supported by good wood, is quite stable and your body functions work well. Your only weakness is the way you handle anger. Anger can be healthy when it lets you know what you do or don't want, but it can be harmful to your liver if you repress it.

## SPECIAL MESSAGES

### If you see a green woodpecker

You have intimate ties with your soul family, and this link is just as precious as your connection with your birth family.

### If you hear a green woodpecker

It is up to you to build your tomorrow in the image of what you want it to be. Don't expect someone else to do it for you. Your vision is unique, and it is your duty to participate in the unfolding transformation.

## If you find a green woodpecker's feather
You are connected with your earthly and spiritual essence, and this balance is enabling you to make your way serenely towards the future.

# Zebra

Element: **earth**

Season: **summer**

Keywords: **duality, atypical personality, difference**

With their black and white stripes, zebras speak about duality. Each zebra has a different stripe pattern, and this power animal invites you to accept the positive and negative aspects of your personality to reveal your uniqueness. Individuality is a gift you give yourself.

## MESSAGE

You are unique, so don't be afraid to be different. There is no one like you, and your singular character is very much a part of your appeal. The world needs people who take ownership of themselves, so bring out everything you've got to shine in this world!

# Legendary animals

# Centaur

Element: **earth**

Season: **summer**

Keywords: **desires, drive, primal energy**

Half-man and half-horse, the centaur represents your ability to accept your animal side, that part of yourself that releases impulses and primal desires that are incredible sources of energy. We all dream of being quicker, stronger and better looking and to be able to cross our own lines and explore new horizons as though we had pulled on a pair of seven-league boots.

## MESSAGE

Humans are animals like any other and the centaur invites you to let that part of you that carries wilder desires and impulses express itself. If you're willing to be a part of the animal kingdom you'll find the strength that resides in these primitive energies. The centaur's energy is very sexual, and you might have needs in that area that deserve to be heard. Become aware that the act of love comes from the joining of two bodies, but also of two souls.

# Dragon

Element: **fire**
Season: **summer**
Keywords: **transmutation, protection, gentleness**

Dragons are fantastic beings that live in invisible realms alongside humans, protecting them and their living spaces. You can invite a dragon's energy into your home to maintain its good vibes. The dragon's energy is gentle, contrary to what you might believe, as these extraordinary beings are filled with love and compassion and know how to use their luminous fire to transmute negative energies.

## MESSAGE

The comfort of your home is like a log fire that must be kept alive. Remember to regularly clean the energies that have accumulated in your living space. You can also bring light into it through the use of crystals, intentions and prayer and, why not: you could even invite a dragon to watch over it.

# Griffin

Element: **fire**

Season: **winter**

Keywords: **life mission, contribution, extrasensory abilities**

Griffins embody multiple energies, of the lion, eagle and horse. They are treasure guardians, and they watch over people's talents and extrasensory abilities. The griffin can see the rough diamond in the heart of every human, a diamond that needs to be refined and protected from ill-intentioned people. Your gifts are presents from the heavens. The griffin is sent to you to help you discover and fulfil your mission on earth.

## MESSAGE

You may not have yet discovered your calling in this life. If the griffin appears to you it could be because you have extrasensory capacities waiting for you to be ready to explore them. Embrace the griffin's message, as this power animal has come to help you on your path of awakening.

# Hydra

Element: **earth**

Season: **autumn**

Keywords: **immortality, light, healing**

Hydras embody the healing and deep transformation energy of the snake (see page 290) but multiplied by its many heads. The hydra's capacity for constant regeneration along with its immortality are a source of fascination for humans, who try to kill it as though life could only have meaning because we are destined to die and any animal spared this end is necessarily evil. This archetype is related to the fact that humans are unaware of the immortal nature of their own souls, and therefore fear their own deaths.

## MESSAGE

Being born means accepting that one day you will die. When as a human you become aware of both your light and shadow parts you will realise that your soul is an immortal form of energy. The hydra wants to help you release your fear of death by showing you that you can be constantly reborn to yourself throughout this life and in your lives to come. Wherever there are shadows there is also light, and vice versa. If you can understand this principle you will be able to find your light.

# Phoenix

Element: **fire**

Season: **summer**

Keywords: **immortality, the soul, sacredness**

Phoenixes have the ability to be reborn from their ashes, thus representing your immortality. The phoenix comes to heal your soul of its fear of death by attempting to show you your sacred and divine nature. The phoenix resonates with the energy of life cycles, which you must accept, and supports you in your life changes and in the passing of your loved ones.

## MESSAGE

Deceased loved ones, human or animal, are watching over you. They still exist but in other forms, and by realising how you are guided and supported you can heal the feelings of loneliness and fear that sometimes rise up within you. The phoenix comes to reveal your light, the one that will continue to shine even after your passing. No one ever really leaves us, as the ones you loved on earth are still there right beside you!

# Siren

Element: **water**
Season: **spring**
Keywords: **birth, breath, incarnation**

Sirens possess hypnotic voices that lead men who encounter them to lose touch with reality, and they open the doors of their water realm to them. These half-woman and half-fish beings are connected with the 'Aum', the creative sound of the universe that programs all DNA. The siren's call brings the water in your cells into vibration as though to trigger a rebirth and give you a second wind to enter life in full awareness.

## MESSAGE

The siren evokes the first breath of life, your first cry in this world. If you can't seem to make your ideas heard then the siren is offering you a second birth. Breathe in deeply, and change the inner program that keeps your voice locked on earth. You have a unique vibe, so don't doubt your incarnation. You are where you are meant to be.

# Unicorn

Element: **spirit**

Season: **spring**

Keywords: **imagination, dreams, freedom**

The unicorn embodies the qualities of the horse (see page 153), such as bringing things into harmony and releasing limiting beliefs associated with the magic of imaginary realms. As in *The Wizard of Oz* and *Alice in Wonderland*, the unicorn brings the gift of a dream realm in which your imagination is set free. The unicorn invites you to free your creativity so you can let it express itself without constraint.

## MESSAGE

Thoughts and creation are conditioned by fashion and standards. The unicorn urges you to recapture your freedom of imagination and creation. Creativity does not necessarily mean art; it also signifies designing your world in the way of your dreams!

# Dual
# animals

**BULLFROG:** *believe in your dreams*

Bullfrogs are the biggest frogs in Europe. Regulators of ravaging insect populations, they are the guardians of calm waters. The bullfrog possesses the bull's leadership qualities, as well as the transformation abilities of the frog. This power animal invites you to bring your dreams into reality without letting yourself be polluted by the outer world.

**CATFISH:** *you will receive guidance*

If you come across one of these whiskered fish it means you are invited to dive with it into the realm of intuition. Set aside an evening and settle down for a meditation session, because you will receive guidance in one form or another!

**GREATER STAG BEETLE:** *your spirit guide is with you*

With their mandibles built like a stag's antlers, greater stag beetles are the most majestic members of the beetle order, with an incredible connection to celestial energies. When you meet one it is a sign that your spirit guide or a deceased loved one is with you.

**LADYBIRD SPIDER:** *bringer of good luck*

Ladybird spiders look like bright spiders dressed up as ladybirds, as though they wanted to foil their destiny by taking on a fun appearance to scare people. Ladybird spiders bring good fortune, so if you are lucky enough to see one it means that good news awaits you and that life has a surprise in store for you.

**LOP (RAM) RABBIT:** *dare to venture out*

Lop (ram) rabbits are able to overcome their condition and venture into new territories. Their message is: 'Don't be afraid to change horizons!' With a little willpower you can release the fears that prevent you from fulfilling your deep potential.

**PARROT FISH:** *own your uniqueness*

This animal's name is a perfect reflection of its highly colourful appearance. When the parrot fish appears to you it is an invitation to own your originality. You are a singular human being, and your difference is a treasure.

**RHINOCEROS BEETLE:** *a delicate choice is before you*

This beetle's particularity is that it sports a horn on the front of its head like a rhino's. This power animal has come to alert you to the importance of a choice that is before you. Don't rush into it! The rhinoceros beetle urges you to look at the situation from every angle before making a decision, as there may be a problem hidden somewhere.

**TIGER MOSQUITO:** *balance out your duality*

The tiger mosquito's sting is more redoubtable than that of its western cousin, as though it wanted you to keep in mind that you cannot live in a world made only of pleasure. When this power animal crashes the party it is to remind you that duality is everywhere, and that there are always two sides to everything in life. By remaining aware of this you can appreciate shared moments as ephemeral joys that should be experienced fully.

**TIGER SHARK:** *what is your anger telling you?*

The shark's initiation energy associated with the tiger's inner fire underscores an anger issue that you need to overcome. Why repress your anger? The tiger shark invites you to accept each feeling as a part of your earthly experience. Don't reject what anger can teach you, such as becoming aware of your limits and setting boundaries.

**WHALE SHARK:** *peacemaker*

The whale shark is the biggest fish in the world, but it is also an eminent peacemaker. It possesses the energy of mediation and conflict resolution. With its ties to the shark's forward-moving energy and the wisdom of the whale, this power animal invites you to take on the role of adviser and helper. When you use your social skills you will find your place.

### WOLF DOG: *listen to your instinct*
Wolf dogs are a cross between domesticated dogs and wolves, and have a half-docile and half-wild instinct. When you encounter the wolf dog it is to remind you that there is a wild person inside you too who needs to find their place in so-called civilised society. You are invited to listen more deeply to your instinct.

### WOLF SPIDER: *enlightened mother*
These spiders carry their babies on their backs and are very protective creatures. When this power animal comes to you it is to speak about your role as a parent: how can you give your children enough freedom to allow their creativity to be expressed while providing them with the security they need? The wolf spider invites you to call upon your resources to invent the parenthood that looks like you.

# Acknowledgements

To everyone who agreed to have their story included in this book, thank you for helping to make it so vibrantly alive.

To the animals who came to assist me in the writing of the book through surprising and perfect synchronicities, thank you.

To the everyday magic that makes life so exciting, thank you.

## About the author

Aurore Pramil is a healer, shaman, alchemist and animal interpreter. She has the ability to hear the voices of all kinds of animals and to communicate with them. High on a mountain an eagle once led her on an initiatory path, leading her to discover her unique talents.

Parler-aux-animaux.fr | ⬤ ecole_com_animale

## About the illustrator

Thiago Bianchini is an illustrator and graphic designer. He started drawing at age 14, creating his first works of art at 16 when he painted longboard decks for a skateboard shop. Using mainly black and white illustrations, he focuses on nature, human feelings and a new way of looking at our world. He passionately feels that nature and art are connected.

Thiagobianchini.com | ⬤ thiago_bianchini